A Parent's Guide® to
Southeastern Michigan

parent's guide press

Los Angeles, CA
www.pgpress.com

Heidi Rehak Lovy

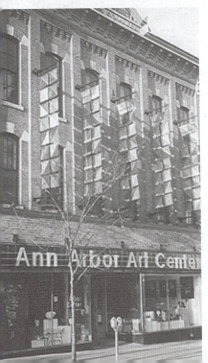

A Parent's Guide® to
Southeastern Michigan

Text and Maps © Mars Publishing 2003

ISBN: 1-931199-25-6

Mars Publishing and the Mars Publishing Logo, Parent's Guide and the Parent's Guide logo are trademarks of Mars Publishing, Inc. The author and Mars Publishing have tried to make the information in this book as accurate as possible. We accept no responsibility for any loss, injury, or inconvenience sustained by anyone using this book.

This book, and all titles in the Parent's Guide series, are available for purposes of fund raising and educational sales to charity drives, fund raisers, parent or teacher organizations, schools, government agencies and corporations at a discount for purchases of more than 10 copies. Persons or organizations wishing to inquire should call Mars Publishing at 1-800-549-6646 or write to us at *sales@marspub.com*.

At the time of publication of this book, all of the information contained within was correct to the best of our knowledge. If you find information in this book that has changed, please contact us. Even better, if you have additional places to recommend, please let us know. Any included submissions to the new edition of this book will get the submitter a by-line in the book and a free copy of any Mars publication.

Please contact us at *parentsguides@marspub.com*

Printed in Singapore.

DEDICATION

This book is dedicated with much love to my parents, Diane and Fred Rehak, who exposed me early on to many of Michigan's natural wonders. And to my husband, Howard, who, along with his two daughters Sonya and Sarah, has given me a completely new perspective on having fun in this great state.

parent's guide press

Edwin E. Steussy, CEO and Publisher
Dianne Tangel-Cate, Project Editor
Anna-Lisa Fay, Editor
Lars H. Peterson, Acquisitions Editor
Michael P. Duggan, Graphic Artist

PO Box 401736, Los Angeles CA 90048

Table of Contents

contents

Southeastern Michigan

Introduction

A Parent's Guide to Southeastern Michigan is a unique handbook for families who are driven to explore the Motor City and its surrounding environs. As a stepparent and lifelong Michiganian, I plan to take you on a cruise of the area, offering up thoughtful, easy-to-use tips for enjoying the region's well-known attractions, while also helping you find and enjoy those half-hidden gems and activities that make Detroit a terrific place to visit. The must-see sites—like The Henry Ford, America's Greatest History Attraction—are highlighted here with the family in mind, as are the not-so-obvious sites, like the spectacular views from the Detroit People Mover.

Detroit is the sixth largest city in the country, yet despite its size, many tourists hold fast to its unfortunate reputation of years past. This book will help dispel any lingering negativity and feature Detroit's many unique neighborhoods and surrounding natural wonders. Depart from downtown Detroit, and Southeastern Michigan transforms quickly: from suburban sprawl to the rolling hills and lakes of northern Oakland County and the arts-oriented climate of Ann Arbor, home of the University of Michigan.

Whether you're planning a day trip to the area, a weekend excursion, or a longer stay, all you need is an enthusiastic family, a form of transportation, and this book to guide you through the many activities Detroit and Southeastern Michigan have to offer. Even those already familiar with the region will discover original and intriguing adventures, complete with these recommendations for entertainment, educational activities, indoor and outdoor fun, and ideas on how to entertain the family regardless of the season or weather.

Introduction

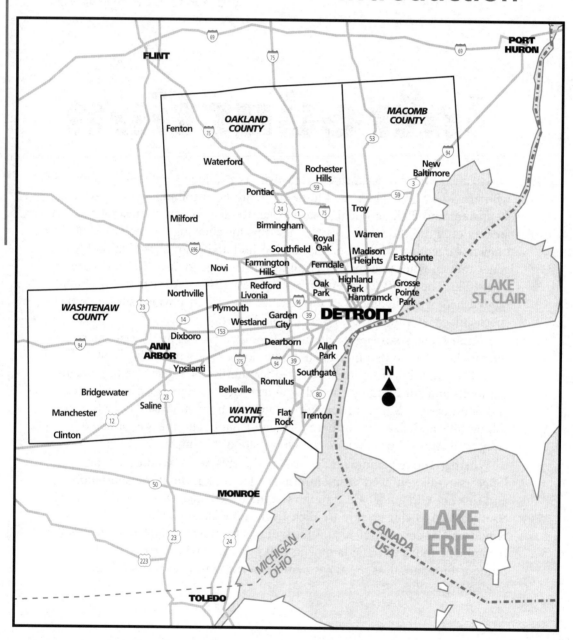

Introduction

I have lived in Michigan all of my thirty-some years, and in the Metro Detroit area for the last twelve years. My parents are outdoor enthusiasts, and practically since birth, I've hiked and camped all over the state. As a teenager, this wasn't always the most exciting vacation prospect, but I came to appreciate being exposed to the great outdoors and eventually found myself imbued with a profound respect for nature.

Attending college in the heart of Detroit's Cultural Center allowed for a much-needed big-city experience. I loved that I could leave the center of downtown Detroit, drive thirty minutes, and come upon rolling hills, majestic woods, and cool lakes. And over the last few years, I've rediscovered much of the area, from downtown Detroit to the woods of Northern Michigan, through the eyes of my two stepdaughters. My career as a reporter and editor for various local newspapers, and as a public relations and special events coordinator for several social service organizations, has broadened my intimate knowledge of the area. I also plan one of the area's largest art fairs, which features a fabulous children's area, if I do say so myself.

It's with this background, and a love for the area, that I hope to enlighten travelers to this region with a guide to making the most of your trip. I've tried to steer away from major chains to ensure that your time spent in Southeastern Michigan is as unique as the area itself. As with life, things change often in business, so please call ahead whenever possible to confirm hours of operation and costs.

Introduction

How to Use This Book

Chapter One will deal with the things you need to know in order to get the most out of your visit to Southeastern Michigan. A brief history of the area is followed by a section on the area as you will find it today. I have also included information on safety, weather, driving, local media, saving money, some of my favorite websites that highlight the area, and a list of community centers and recreation departments.

Chapters Two, Three, Four, and Five are a county-by-county listing of things to do, see, buy, and eat with your family. Through each chapter, I have divided activities under the following categories: "Just for Fun," including walkable downtowns, markets, shops, theaters, tours, and sports; "Parking It," for all things related to parks and the outdoors; and "For Inquisitive Minds," which includes museums, science centers, and other brain-stimulating stuff. Chapter Two includes a special "Distinctly Detroit" section of attractions you simply won't find anywhere else.

Chapter Six focuses on day and weekend trips. Keeping in mind that your visit to Southeastern Michigan may be brief, I've suggested trips that can be made in two hours or less. But for those who have more time to spend and are interested in exploring the rest of the Mitten State and beyond, you'll find listings of things to do in central, northern, and western Michigan that will require driving five hours or less. And for the heck of it, I've included a few out-of-state options as well.

Finally, you'll find a calendar of regional annual events and a supplemental area directory.

Southeastern Michigan

Chapter One

Background

Before the arrival of the first white man, Michigan was inhabited by various Native American tribes, including the Ojibwa (also called the Chippewa), Ottawa, and Potawatomi. In 1701, French Army officer and trader Antoine de la Mothe Cadillac (1658–1730) stumbled upon what is now Detroit and established a settlement at the waterway between Lakes St. Claire and Erie.

Cadillac convinced King Louis XIV's chief minister, Count Pontchartrain, that a permanent community at this strategic location would strengthen French control over the upper Great Lakes and repel British advances. Not to mention that the area was a perfect spot from which to send furs to Canada. So Cadillac built Fort Pontchartrain, but it was not enough to keep the British away.

The French lost the fort in 1760 during the French and Indian War. The British, who now occupied the region, preserved the area's given French names (without actually understanding them). That is why the city is called Detroit, meaning "the straits," and the waterway is curiously named the Detroit River (though it is actually a strait).

Had the French been victorious, perhaps the future Motor City would have been named for Cadillac. Instead, Cadillac is a small town in Northern Michigan known primarily as an exporter of Christmas trees.

Chapter One

Cadillac's association with Detroit did not end there, however. When Henry Martyn Leland (1843–1932) founded an automobile company in 1904, he named it the Cadillac Motor Car Company in honor of the city's founder. In fact, that's the Cadillac family crest you see prominently displayed on the back of the luxury cars.

After American independence, Detroit became part of the Northwest Territory and was incorporated as a town in 1802. Three years later, a fire destroyed 299 of the town's 300 buildings. Territorial Governor Judge Augustus Woodward laid out a plan to rebuild the city, featuring public squares and circular parks, based on models of Washington, D.C., and Paris.

Woodward also planned to widen the Saginaw Trail, a Native American route for transporting furs that ran about twenty-eight miles north from the Detroit River. Now known as Woodward Avenue (or M-1), this six-lane main artery from Detroit to the northern suburbs has been designated a "Michigan Heritage Route" (see www.woodwardheritage.com for more than 300 historical sites to be found along the avenue). "Woodwarding" became a craze in the 1950s and '60s as teens discovered the thrill of taking Dad's car out for a spin along the strip and to drive-through burger joints. Even now, muscle cars—and just about every other form of wheeled, motorized vehicle you can imagine—reappear en masse every August for the Woodward Dream Cruise, an event that draws more than one million people (see Page 164).

Pre-car Detroit was an important station along the Underground Railroad, a network of escape routes set up by abolitionists for slaves who traveled from America's southern states north into Canada. Said to have been in place as early as the colonial period, the Underground Railroad reached its height of activity between 1830 and 1865. Detroit was a major escape route because of its proximity to the Canadian border. The John Freeman Walls Historic Site and Underground Railroad Museum in Windsor, Ontario, honors the more than 40,000 slaves who found freedom through this network.

Background

Putting the World on Wheels

In the 1850s, Detroit began building railroad cars, ships, and stoves, and major industries were established that exploited Michigan's vast resources of iron ore, copper, and water. The population surged from about 2,200 in 1830 to approximately 80,000 in 1870.

When the first automobiles were seen tooling down city streets in the late 1890s, Detroit's main industry was stovemaking. But Michigan was a leading producer of carriages, buggies, wheels, and bicycles, and Detroit was already making marine gas engines. Its access to water gave it an industrial advantage because freighters could ship raw materials such as iron ore from northern areas. Still, the automobile made little impact on the city at first, for most people believed it would never replace the bicycle or the horse.

Ransom E. Olds (1864–1950) started Michigan's first auto company in 1900, and by 1905 Olds Motor Works was churning out 6,500 cars annually. In 1908, however, a farmer's son, named Henry Ford (1863–1947), built the first Model T, and cars quickly became popular. In 1914, Ford ran the first conveyer-belt assembly line at his factory in Highland Park, offering the unheard-of wage of five dollars a day for eight hours' work. By 1921, Ford had produced more than five million cars. The city's population reached nearly one million people, as workers from the South, across the country, and throughout the world came for jobs in the automobile plants.

Along with the development of mass-production methods came the growth of the labor movement. In the 1930s, when the automobile industry was well established in the state, labor unions struggled for recognition. The conflict between labor and the automotive industry, which continued into the 1940s, included sit-down strikes and sometimes more violent protests. Walter Reuther (1907–1970), a pioneer of the labor movement, was elected president of the United Auto Workers (UAW) in 1946. Driven by the automobile's success, Detroit was the first city to have a paved concrete road (in 1909), the first to install a traffic light (in 1915), and the first to build an urban freeway in the United States (in 1942).

Chapter One

Paving Its Way

The 1920s were a time of unprecedented prosperity for Detroit. The booming city was a glimmering example of American opportunity. For decades, it boasted the highest percentage of home ownership in the nation. Huge, ornate theaters were built downtown for movies and stage shows. The J. L. Hudson department store was one of the world's largest and most famous. The city developed a superb system of streetcars and trolleys. Belle Isle became one of the most beautiful urban parks in the nation. The Ambassador Bridge and the Detroit-Windsor Tunnel were built to link Detroit to Canada. Navin Field (later known as Briggs Stadium and then Tiger Stadium) became one of the nation's most acclaimed sporting venues.

During the Prohibition Era, a thriving underground business developed as mobsters shipped liquor across the waters from Canada. The Great Depression of the 1930s hit Detroit hard initially, but the automobile industry survived.

During World War II, the auto companies converted their factories in short order to the production of planes and tanks. The war effort was centered around Willow Run Airport in Washtenaw County, and the Edsel Ford Expressway was built between downtown Detroit and the airport to facilitate that work. It was the nation's first great freeway—but a smaller example, the Davison, had opened a few years previously in Detroit and Highland Park.

Major shifts occurred in Detroit's demographics after World War II. The post-war economic boom was accompanied by the construction of a network of freeways that decimated Detroit's old neighborhoods, while making possible the exponential growth of suburbs. For a while, downtown Detroit remained the thriving center of the metropolitan area, and its population peaked at 2.1 million in the late 1950s.

Background

On the Road to Success

It was a former autoworker who led the way for Detroit's other famous twentieth-century contribution—Motown. Founded by Berry Gordy Jr. in 1959 with an $800 loan, the upstart record company introduced the world to Marvin Gaye, Stevie Wonder, Smokie Robinson, Michael Jackson, the Temptations, Diana Ross, and others—all of whom either grew up in or gained their first fame in Detroit. You can tour the original recording studio, "Hitsville U.S.A," when you visit the Motown Historical Museum (see Page 42).

As more prosperous people fled the city in the early 1960s and left poorer ones behind, racial tensions heightened. They exploded during the infamous 1967 riots, which left dozens dead and hastened the so-called white flight. The city plunged into a long decline, as key components of business, industry, and culture shifted to the suburbs. Even football's Detroit Lions left Tiger Stadium to move to a new stadium in Pontiac.

Civic leaders made efforts to turn things around, starting with the building of the Renaissance Center office-hotel-retail complex in 1973. But for years, the Renaissance Center remained an isolated fortress with little effect on surrounding areas. The city kept losing people and money, and its fine housing stock suffered from neglect and abandonment. The automobile industry was hit hard by a severe recession caused by rising oil prices and competition from Japanese imports. Factories in the city closed, and thousands of good-paying jobs for unskilled workers disappeared.

But the metropolitan area continued to grow and thrive, and downtown's resurgence took halting steps. In the 1980s, Joe Louis Arena was constructed as the home of the Detroit Red Wings hockey team. The Millender Center opened near the Renaissance Center. Red Wings and Tigers owner (and Little Caesar's pizza king) Mike Ilitch saved the Fox Theatre, and its revival began a genuine downtown resurgence in the 1990s. Through that decade, Detroiters debated the merits of casinos and a new baseball stadium, finally approving both ideas. During the 1990s, the city's population stabilized at around a million people, and business investment began returning to the city.

Chapter One

Detroit Today

Today's Southeastern Michigan is in transition. City leaders in Detroit are looking to casinos and two new professional sports venues to draw consumers to downtown. The growth of the suburbs has permanently changed the region's landscape. Many jobs, hotels, restaurants, shopping centers, and entertainment facilities are now outside the city limits, creating a sprawling metropolitan area that remains heavily dependent on the automobile.

Yet a more unified approach to the area's problems and prospects has civic leaders optimistic. Detroit retains its rich cultural gems, its vibrant entertainment and dining scene, and above all, its strength as a genuine melting pot—with immigrants from around the world bringing their own cuisine, traditions, and religions. It has proven to be a resilient place—and one of America's greatest, and perhaps most overlooked, cities.

The Metropolitan Detroit area—which includes Wayne, Oakland, and Macomb counties—has a population of just more than four million people, about 951,000 of whom live within the Detroit city limits.

The ever-expanding 203-acre Wayne State University is Michigan's only urban research university, located smack-dab in the middle of the city's University Cultural Center. The university's fourteen schools offer more than 350 major subject areas to more than 31,000 graduate and undergraduate students.

In 1997, the Charles H. Wright Museum of African American History opened the doors to its new 120,000-square-foot facility close to the Wayne State campus. With its state-of-the-art digs, lectures, exhibits, and festivals, it's the largest museum of its kind in the world (see Page 35 for more info).

Metro Detroit is home to the global headquarters for four of the world's top automakers: General Motors Corp., Ford Motor Co., DaimlerChrysler AG, and Volkswagen of America. The region also ranks as a leader in the production of paints, nonelectrical machinery, and automation equipment in pharmaceutical, rubber products, synthetic resins, and garden seed.

Background

Safety Information

The best tip that can be passed along when traveling here—and anywhere, for that matter—is to use common sense. Obviously you shouldn't hang out with your family after dark in certain areas, and flashing your wallet around probably isn't a good idea in most places. Areas that were once completely unsafe for visitors, like the Cass Corridor and Brush Park, are now being rebuilt, but it's still probably best to visit during the day.

Unfortunately, however, there are still locales in the Detroit area that just aren't too safe. Downtown Detroit, for example, isn't as walkable as San Francisco. Once you're in Greektown, it isn't a good idea to walk to the Theatre District with your kids. If you attend a baseball game at Comerica Park, don't walk to Rivertown for dinner; drive. It's best to travel to the different neighborhoods in your car.

Use the same logic you'd apply in other large cities. Avoid deserted areas, especially at night, and don't go into public parks after dark unless there's a concert or similar occasion that will attract a crowd. Avoid carrying valuables with you on the street, and don't display expensive cameras or electronic equipment. Hold onto your pocketbook, and place your billfold in an inside pocket. In theaters, restaurants, and other public places, keep your possessions in sight.

Remember also that hotels are open to the public, and in a large hotel, security might not be able to screen everyone entering. Always lock your room door; don't assume that once you're inside your hotel, you no longer need to be aware of your surroundings. And make sure your children know the name of your hotel.

Driving safety is important, too. Ask the rental agency for written directions to your destination, or a map with the route clearly marked. If possible, arrive and depart during daylight hours.

If you drive off a highway into a dubious neighborhood, leave the area as quickly as possible. If you have an accident, even on the highway, stay in your car with the doors locked until you assess the situation or until the police arrive. If you're bumped from behind or are involved in a minor accident with no injuries and the situation appears to be suspicious, do not get out of your car. Motion to the other driver to follow you to the nearest well-lit service station or twenty-four–hour store to report the accident.

Always try to park in illuminated, well-traveled areas. If you leave your rental car unlocked and devoid of your valuables, you're probably safer than if you were to lock your car with valuables in plain view. If someone attempts to rob you or steal your car, don't try to resist. Report the incident to the police immediately by calling 911.

Chapter One

Weather

It's likely not a coincidence that the state of Michigan is shaped like a mitten—you'll definitely need them if you travel here between October and April. Make sure you pack plenty of clothing to keep your family warm and dry if you're traveling here during the winter months. Snowfall averages about 70 inches but can easily climb to more than 100 inches, depending on where you are. Summer temperatures are generally in the 80°F range, with a fair amount of humidity. Annual rainfall averages 30 inches per year.

Climate: Average high and low temperatures (°F/°C):

Month	High	Low	Month	High	Low
January	31/-1	16/-9	July	83/29	61/16
February	34/1	18/-8	August	82/28	59/15
March	44/7	27/-3	September	74/24	52/17
April	58/15	37/3	October	63/17	41/5
May	69/21	47/8	November	48/9	31/-1
June	79/26	56/13	December	35/2	22/6

Driving Tips

It's important to remember that the Detroit area is built by and for automobiles. Navigating the area is fairly easy, and parking is usually a breeze. Rush hour on local freeways starts early. Be patient if you need to drive anytime from 6:30 to 9:00 a.m., and later in the day from 4:00 to 6:00 p.m. You'll undoubtedly find yourself on one of the main arteries through Southeastern Michigan, including I-696, which runs east and west, and I-75, which runs north and south.

Accidents or snowstorms can quickly back up highways for miles, so I suggest hopping on one of the "mile" roads if you're headed east or west, or Woodward Avenue, Telegraph Road, or one of the other secondary streets that run north and south.

Starting at Ford Road, which is essentially 0 Mile Road, the east and west streets are found at one-mile intervals. Warren Avenue is 1 Mile Road, McNichols is 6 Mile Road, and Maple Road is 15 Mile Road. The roads were originally based on the numbers of miles from the intersection of Michigan and Woodward Avenues in downtown Detroit. Detroiters frequently use these mile roads as a quick reference when giving directions.

Background

If you plan on traveling to Canada during rush hour or on weekends and holidays, expect significant delays at the Detroit-Windsor Tunnel and the Ambassador Bridge. It is recommended that you have passports for the adults in your car and birth certificates for any minors when you go through customs.

Local Media

Daily Newspapers

The Detroit News (www.detnews.com)

Detroit Free Press (www.freep.com)

The Oakland Press (www.oakpress.com)

Weekly Newspapers

Metro Times (available for free at area businesses and bookstores, or at www.MetroTimes.com)

Metro Parent Magazine (available for free at area bookstores)

Selected Radio Stations

WDET (101.9-FM) — Detroit Public Radio, National Public Radio

WJR (760-AM) — News, talk

WWJ (950-AM) — News, talk

WUOM (91.7-FM) — Ann Arbor Public Radio, National Public Radio

WCSX (94.7-FM) — Classic Rock

CIMX (88.7) — Alternative Rock

WWWW (102.9) — Country

WOMC (104.3) — Oldies

WJLB (97.9) — Hip hop

WDRQ (93.1) — Top 40

Television Stations

WJBK-TV (Channel 2) — Fox affiliate

WDIV-TV (Channel 4) — NBC affiliate

WXYZ-TV (Channel 7) — ABC affiliate

CBC-TV (Channel 9) — Canadian Broadcasting Corp.

WKBD-TV (Channel 50) — UPN affiliate

WTVS-TV (Channel 56) — Public Television

WWJ-TV (Channel 62) — CBS affiliate

Chapter One

Cost-Saving Tips

Research the Internet: Many local museums offer specials, like "Grandparent's Day" or other themed discounts. Call ahead or check the website for special promotions. Also, use keywords "discount," "Detroit," and "tourism" to see what deals you can come up with on tours, hotels, events, and restaurants.

Give Entertainment® books a try: Each edition of the book contains thousands of dollars in 50-percent–off and "two-for-one" discount offers from local and national restaurants, hotels, and other merchants specializing in leisure activities. In the Detroit book, you'll find hundreds of coupons for significant discounts at local restaurants, museums, theaters, and recreational centers. Call (888) 231-SAVE, or check out the website at **www.entertainment.com**. At $35, the book can easily pay for itself in a weekend.

Important Contacts

Ambulance/Fire/Emergency: 911
Highway Information: **www.mdot.state.mi.us/laneclosure/**
Detroit Poison Control Center: (313) 745-5711
Children's Hospital of Michigan: (313) 745-5437
Detroit Metropolitan Airport: 734-AIRPORT; **www.metroairport.com**

Recommended Websites

www.cbdfdestinationdetroit.org
   (Central Business District Foundation magazine)
www.visitdetroit.com (Detroit Metro Convention and Visitor's Bureau)
www.annarbor.org (Ann Arbor Area Convention and Visitor's Bureau)
www.michigan.org (State of Michigan's official site)
www.digitalcity.com/detroit (America Online guide to the area)

Background

Community Centers and Recreation Departments

Since Michigan temperatures and weather are extreme—from excruciatingly cold, snowy winters to sticky, humid summers—sometimes it's nice to have an indoor place to burn off some energy. The following community centers and recreation departments offer a variety of programs, classes, and workshops of interest to families. Nominal charges may apply to nonresidents; I'd recommend calling ahead.

Berkley Community Center
2400 Robina Avenue
Berkley, MI 48072
(248) 546-2450

Bloomfield Hills Recreation Department
4200 Andover Road
Bloomfield Hills, MI 48302
(248) 433-0885

Butzel Family Center
7737 Kercheval Street
Detroit, MI 48214
(313) 852-4734

Clinton Township Parks and Recreation
40700 Romeo Plank Road
Clinton Township, MI 48038
(586) 286-9336

Coleman A. Young Community Center
2751 Robert Bradby Drive
Detroit, MI 48207
(313) 877-8008

Farmington Activities Center
28600 11 Mile Road
Farmington Hills, MI 48336
(248) 473-1816

Ford Community and Performing Arts Center
15801 Michigan Avenue
Dearborn, MI 48126
(313) 943-2350

Gerry Kulick Community Center
1201 Livernois
Ferndale, MI 48220
(248) 544-6767

Hazel Park Recreation Department
620 Woodward Heights
Hazel Park, MI 48030
(248) 547-5535

Hunter Community Center
509 Fisher Court
Clawson, MI 48017
(248) 589-0334

Jewish Community Center of Washtenaw County
2935 Birch Hollow Drive
Ann Arbor, MI 48108
(734) 971-0990

Jewish Community Center
15110 W. 10 Mile Road
Oak Park, MI 48237
(248) 967-4030

Jewish Community Center
6600 W. Maple Road
West Bloomfield, MI 48322
(248) 661-1000

Meri Lou Murray Recreation Center
2960 Washtenaw Avenue
Ann Arbor, MI 48104
(734) 971-6337, ext. 2

Oak Park Community Center
14300 Oak Park Boulevard
Oak Park, MI 48237
(248) 691-7555

Olds-Robb Student Recreation Center
Eastern Michigan University
100 Olds-Robb Street
Ypsilanti, MI 48197
(734) 487-1338

Parkridge Community Center
591 Armstrong Drive
Ypsilanti, MI 48197
(734) 996-3056

Pleasant Ridge Community Center
4 Ridge Road
Pleasant Ridge, MI 48069
(248) 542-7322

Roseville Recreation Center
18185 Sycamore Street
Roseville, MI 48066
(586) 445-5480

Royal Oak Community Center
3500 Marais Avenue
Royal Oak, MI 48073
(248) 246-3180

Southfield Sports Arena
26000 Evergreen Road
Southfield, MI 48076
(248) 354-9357

Troy Community Center
3179 Livernois Road
Troy, MI 48083
(248) 524-3484

Warren Community Center
5460 Arden Avenue
Warren, MI 48092
(586) 268-8400

Ypsilanti Township Recreation Center
2025 E. Clark Road
Ypsilanti, MI 48198
(734) 544-3800

Chapter Two

Wayne County

From the heart of Detroit to some of the swankiest suburbs in the United States, Wayne County has many faces. Located in Southeastern Michigan, encompassing approximately 623 square miles, Wayne County is made up of thirty-three cities, ten townships, one village, and forty-one public school districts. Its population of approximately 2.1 million makes it the most largely populated county in Michigan and the eighth most populous county in the nation. Demographically, residents are about 52 percent Caucasian, 42 percent African American, and 2 percent Asian. Its largest employers are Ford Motor Co., General Motors Corp., DaimlerChrysler AG, and the Detroit Medical Center.

Michigan's largest city, Detroit, is bordered to the south by the Detroit River, to the north by Eight Mile Road, to the east by Moross Road, and to the west by Telegraph Road. Wayne County's southernmost neighbor is Canada's Windsor, Ontario, which is accessible by the Ambassador Bridge or the Detroit-Windsor Tunnel. Most of us who live within about a thirty-mile radius of the city say we live in "Detroit," not the suburbs of Ferndale or Bloomfield Hills or Southfield, especially when traveling.

Folks who don't live here or who have never been here often react in one of several ways: There may be a furrowed brow followed by a concerned question about gun violence; often a question is posed as to whether my family has a tractor; or finally, someone might ask about the state of the Rust Belt, a somewhat dated term created in the 1970s to describe a bunch of Midwestern states specializing in durable goods. I'm really not exaggerating!

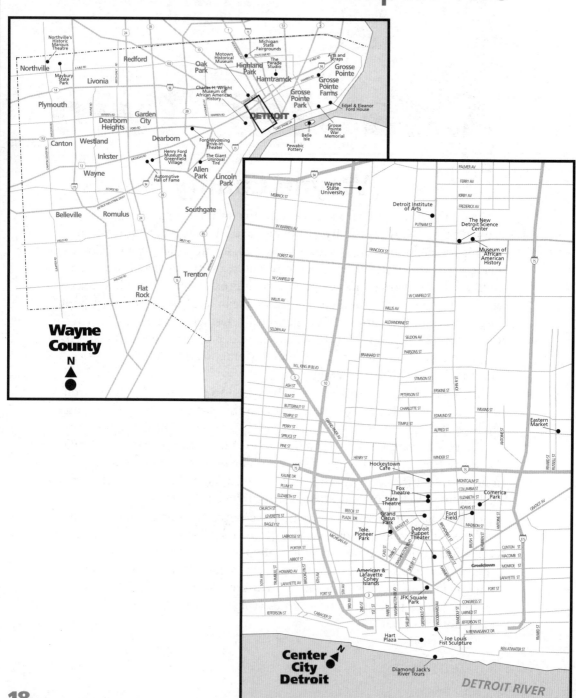

Wayne County

N

Center City Detroit

DETROIT RIVER

Wayne County

While I understand that these reactions are not without some merit, many do not realize that this area is also rich in cultural activities, historic neighborhoods, and world-class sports teams. What's most interesting about the county, however, is that families have the luxury of enjoying all the hustle and bustle that the sixth largest city in the United States has to offer, and they have the opportunity to travel just a few minutes and be hiking or boating in the serene surroundings of some of the area's metro parks.

Just for Fun

Greektown

Downtown Detroit, intersection of Monroe and Beaubien Streets

This is invariably a destination for us when family or friends come to visit from out of town. It's a section of Detroit that is always alive with people and vibrant with the sights, sounds, and smells of a bunch of family-friendly restaurants, pastry shops, and ice cream parlors. You'd be hard pressed to find a kid of any age who wasn't at least a little excited when an order of flaming cheese (saganaki) is brought to their table with a waiter's exclamation of "Opa!"

> **Greektown**
>
> Directions: Getting to Greektown is easy by using the Lafayette exit from I-375. Greektown is well connected to downtown attractions and hotels via the elevated light rail Detroit People Mover, and is just a few minutes' walk to Detroit's Theatre District, Ford Field, and Comerica Park.

Every spring, the streets of Greektown close for a decent art fair where more than 100 artists and crafters sell their handmade wares. My stepdaughters, Sonya and Sarah, got a kick out of a graffiti-style portrait that a street artist did for them for a donation—there are often street vendors offering such services, or playing music or selling flowers. Of course, other big draws for this area are one of Detroit's three major casinos and a handful of bars, but it really can be a fun place for the family during the day.

Greektown is historically significant as a traditional center of retailing in downtown Detroit that has served two distinct ethnic groups in its 140-year history. The area has evolved from a pioneer farm, to a German area, and finally to a Greek-flavored commercial zone. The district is composed of a small enclave of late Victorian, two- and three-story commercial buildings, industrial structures, and churches surrounded by modern structures. Many changes have occurred to these storefronts as various merchants have attempted to customize their buildings with Greek columns and other structural facades more indicative of what's inside today.

Chapter Two

Religious Centers

Greektown is anchored by three historic churches. **Second Baptist Church**, 441 Monroe Street, was founded in 1836 by former slaves, and was an important "station" on the Underground Railroad; **Old St. Mary's Catholic Church**, 646 Monroe Street, blends Pisan Romanesque and Venetian Renaissance details to create one of Detroit's most beautiful churches; and the **Annunciation Greek Orthodox Cathedral**, 707 E. Lafayette, has been at the center of the Greek community since the congregation was founded in 1910.

Restaurants

Greektown's reputation was built on its many famous restaurants. Two of our family's favorite Greek dining spots are the **New Parthenon**, 547 Monroe Street, (313) 963-8888, which can easily accommodate large parties; and **New Hellas Cafe**, 583 Monroe Street, (313) 961-5544, which has a more intimate setting. Both offer some of the most popular Greek dishes, including spanakoteropeta (spinach-cheese pie), lamb chops, and moussaka (layered eggplant and ground lamb with herbs and spices). Other restaurants feature decidedly non-Greek cuisine, such as Cajun and Creole or Chicago-style deep-dish pizza.

Sarah enjoys some sweet treats at Astoria Pastry Shop in Greektown. Photo by Howard Lovy

Historic Trappers Alley, site of Detroit's early fur industry, is now home to one of the three temporary gaming facilities in Detroit, the Greektown Casino, which opened in the fall of 2000. Other notable adaptive reuse projects include the **International Center Building**, 400 Monroe Street, home to the world's largest indoor waterfall (a whopping 114 feet high) and the **Athenaeum Suites Hotel**, Detroit's only AAA-rated, four-diamond hotel.

Wayne County

Mexicantown

(313) 967-9898
www.mexicantown.org

While several Mexican restaurants with a lively ambiance are enough of a draw to take the family to Mexicantown any time of the year, summer months are even more worthwhile. Every Sunday during the summer, merchants host the Mexicantown Summer Mercado (market). Part carnival, part cultural explosion and part market, the Mercado is a free event that features dancing, singing, music, art, clothes, face painting, and more. It's a feast of sights and sounds for the entire family. Pick up a piñata for the kids, some Mexican silver for Mom, and lots of burritos for Dad. It's easy to spend an entire day here.

> **Mexicantown**
>
> Directions: The general area begins 1 block north of the Ambassador Bridge, near Bagley and 21st Streets. Take Exit #48 from I-75 or Exit #191 from I-96.

Eastern Market

2934 Russell Street
Detroit, MI 48207
(313) 833-1560

Detroit's Eastern Market is, simply put, a gem. By early Saturday morning, Russell Street comes alive with a diverse mix of people from the city and the 'burbs—many toting wagons or carts—in search of the freshest fruits, veggies, meat, wine, and flowers. And in the winter, you'll witness families picking out Christmas trees and wreaths brought to the market from local tree farms.

> **Eastern Market**
>
> Hours: 5am–noon, Mon–Fri; 5am–5pm, Sat.
>
> Directions: Exit I-75 at Mack Avenue, head east; south on Russell Street.

What used to be the hub of Detroit's large German community (circa 1880s), today's Eastern Market is home to farmers from Michigan, Ohio, and Canada. The growers sell their goods market style—with plenty of character and care inside the eight open buildings along Russell. The kids love the free samples of mangoes, grapes, and even vegetables offered by sellers. Along the perimeter of the market are several butcher shops and meat processing plants. We try to avoid these areas at all cost, especially since the kids are easily shaken by such things (as am I!)

The market is also known for its annual Flower Day (in early June), a huge plant/flower sale and festival that attracts more than eighty growers. It's the perfect place to take Grandma, Mom, and the kids.

Chapter Two

Sonya and Sarah choose some fruit at Eastern Market.
Photo by Howard Lovy

Don't leave the Eastern Market area without stopping at the Rocky Peanut Company, 1545 Clay Street, (313) 871-5100, **www.rockypeanut.com**. The store roasts fresh nuts every day and features bulk bins of penny candies, nuts, and chocolates that are a big draw for big and small kids alike.

The perfect stop for breakfast or lunch at the market is the ever-packed Russell Street Deli, 2465 Russell Street, (313) 567-2900. It truly makes you feel as if you've stepped into a bustling New York–style deli. Inside the narrow store, lightly colored wood chairs and tables file along the wall across from the stainless steel serving station. Giant sandwiches, piled high, are garnished with gargantuan-sized pickles, and the ingredients couldn't be fresher, since they stock the deli with products from the market right across the street.

The Grosse Pointes

This is the perfect place for a drive during the December holidays if you're interested in checking out some spectacular houses decorated beyond belief. Exquisite mansions line one side of Lake Shore Drive (and Lake St. Clair on the other), and many of those that are viewable from the road will wow the family.

The Village, a downtown shopping district along Kercheval between Neff and Cadieux, is also a fun place to meander with the kids. The Village Toy Company, 16900 Kercheval, (313) 882-1300, is a favorite spot. The store stocks lots of specialty toys you can't find anywhere else. The Village also hosts an annual day-after-Thanksgiving Santa Claus Parade along Kercheval, featuring the "Jingle Bell" walk/run; and Music on the Plaza, a weekly summer event with some of the finest jazz musicians in Michigan performing alfresco on the Village Plaza, at the intersection of Kercheval and St. Clair. People bring picnic baskets and lawn chairs; concerts start at 7:00 p.m.

Wayne County

Grosse Pointe War Memorial

32 Lake Shore Drive
Grosse Pointe Farms, MI 48236
(313) 881-7511

The Grosse Pointe War Memorial is a grand mansion previously owned by the Alger family in the early 1900s. In 1949, the building itself was dedicated to veterans who gave their lives in World War II, to serve as a center for charitable events and continuing education. Today

Grosse Pointe War Memorial

Hours and Cost: Varies per program; call ahead for schedule.

Directions: Exit I-94 at Connor Avenue (#220B), left on Jefferson Avenue, which turns into Lake Shore Drive.

the mansion is used in several ways, from summer concerts on the lake to ballet classes in the lower level of the home. More than 5,000 events are held at the War Memorial annually. Events include lectures, classes, trips, luncheons, and concerts. The building provides a beautiful setting for special events, and many weddings are held here. Some events are open only to residents, so call ahead.

Edsel & Eleanor Ford House

1100 Lake Shore Drive
Grosse Pointe Shores, MI 48236
(313) 884-4222
www.fordhouse.org

Edsel & Eleanor Ford House

Hours: Grounds tours, house tours, and special events vary; call or check website for info.

Cost: Varies by activity.

Directions: Exit I-696 at 11 Mile Road (#28), head east, turn right on Jefferson Avenue, which turns into Lake Shore Drive.

Take an intimate peek at how the family that changed the way we get from here to there lived. The former private residence of Edsel (Henry and Clara Ford's only child) and Eleanor Ford and their children is honestly one of those places where I could live happily in one of the closets. The house alone is exquisite. It was designed by world-renowned architect Albert Kahn and features original paintings by Diego Rivera, Matisse, and Rodin, just to name a few. The grounds are located on a peninsula that juts into Lake St. Clair, and they go on for acres. Kids might find particularly interesting the "Play House," a two-thirds scale Tudor house built in 1930 for Edsel's daughter Josephine on her seventh birthday. The house contains miniature furnishings throughout and is decorated with high-relief stucco characters from nursery rhymes. Cross your fingers that the children don't come away from the Ford House wanting something similar!

Chapter Two

Detroit Puppet Theater

25 E. Grand River Avenue
Detroit, MI 48226
(313) 961-7777
www.puppetart.org

Detroit Puppet Theater

Cost for Saturday performances:
$5, children; $7, adults,
$8 for workshop immediately
following the performance.

Directions: Exit I-94 at Ford Freeway
(#53B), merge onto M-10 at Exit #215A
and merge onto the John C. Lodge
Freeway, take the Grand River Avenue
exit and turn left.

This theater was founded by a group of puppeteers and artists trained in the former Soviet Union. All members of the troupe are masters of puppetry. Even the most jaded teen will probably appreciate the artistry that goes into crafting these works. Little ones may be a bit frightened by the puppets, so it would behoove you to walk around the puppet displays prior to the show. The yearly season includes a different performance each month and incorporates diverse programming, such as "Holiday Month," which features skits on Christmas, Hanukkah, and Kwanzaa.

Fox Theatre

2211 Woodward Avenue
Detroit, MI 48201
(313) 596-3200

Upon encountering the Fox Theatre, with its lion-emblazoned marquee, you witness a regal structure typical of a major metropolis. It's hard to believe that this façade, now a Woodward Avenue landmark, was once at risk. Fashioned in the vaudeville aesthetics of the 1920s, the Fox Theatre was commissioned by movie mogul William Fox to house live theatrical performances and the best the moving pictures had to offer. The theater was the first of Fox's "Temples of Amusement." With an ornate and sumptuous interior reminiscent of the era of gangster flicks, the Fox was the venue in which to see and be seen. From big bands to vaudeville performances, if there was entertainment in Detroit, chances are it was happening here.

Unfortunately, the Detroit of the 1960s was an era that cared little for the flair of this bygone era, and by the 1980s, the Fox narrowly escaped demolition. However, Michael Illitch, chairman and president of Little Caesars

The Fox Theatre lights up Woodward Avenue at night. Photo by Marji Silk

A Parent's Guide to
Southeastern Michigan

Wayne County

Enterprises, came to its rescue. It now stands as a piece of
Detroit history and a testament to the benefits of restora-
tion. The neighborhood surrounding the theater has
enjoyed subsequent revitalization as well.

> **Fox Theatre**
>
> Directions: Exit I-75 at
> Warren Avenue, turn left
> on Woodward Avenue.

As one of the top-grossing theaters of its kind in the
world, the Fox now features Broadway productions, concerts, variety shows,
family entertainment, comedy shows, and classic films, as well as annual favorites,
including *The Radio City Christmas Spectacular*, featuring the "Radio City
Rockettes," "Sesame Street Live!" and "Blue's Clues Live!"

Diamond Jack's River Tours

**Hart Plaza, at the intersection
of Woodward and Jefferson Avenues
Detroit, MI 48226
(313) 843-7676
www.diamondjack.com**

A Detroit River tour is the perfect way to see the city.
Photo courtesy of Detroit Metro Convention & Visitors Bureau

When my stepdaugh-
ter's fifth-grade class
made a field trip out of
a Diamond Jack River
Tour, one of the high-
lights she couldn't wait
to tell us was that "some
kid got in trouble for
throwing trash into the
river." She did, however,
enjoy the scenery quite a
bit, too.

Family owned and
operated Diamond Jack's
River Tours has been
showing off the skylines
of Detroit and Windsor
from a unique vantage point since 1991. Captain Bill Hoey of Grosse Ile, Mich.,
owner and operator of Diamond Jack's and the Gaelic Tugboat Company, was
born in Ferndale, Mich. As a youngster, he spent summers at his uncle's cottage
in northern Canada, which nurtured his interest in boats. The great old steam-

25

boats that plied the Great Lakes captured Hoey's imagination and led to his decision to pursue a career in the maritime industry.

The Diamond Belle, purchased in 1994, and the Diamond Queen, purchased in 1996, are primarily used for private charters and special cruises. All three vessels are U.S. Coast Guard–inspected and –approved annually. Check out the website for special rate tours, and to see the route that takes you from Joe Louis Arena around to sites in Windsor and back to the Ambassador Bridge.

> **Diamond Jack's River Tours**
>
> Cost: 2-hour tours: $14, adults; $12, seniors; $10, children 6–16, under 6 free. Save $2 per ticket with a AAA membership card.
>
> Directions: Depart from Hart Plaza, at the intersection of Woodward and Jefferson Avenues. Exit I-375 at Jefferson Avenue, head west.

Ford Field (home of the Detroit Lions)

2000 Brush Street
Detroit, MI 48226
www.detroitlions.com

The home of the Detroit Lions, Ford Field seats about 65,000.
Photo by Vito Palmisano

While we still need to work on the team, the venue is quite spectacular. The new home to the Lions football team opened in 2002 and features restaurants, shops, and 65,000 seats in its 1.85 million-square-foot field. Ford Field's Adams Street concourse is open daily Monday through Friday from 7:00 a.m. to 4:00 p.m. Visitors can enter Ford Field through Gate A (main entrance at Adams & Brush) or Gate G (southeast entrance on St. Antoine).

En route to other downtown destinations, visit Ah! Mooré, the coffee and pastry shop of former Detroit Lions receiver Herman Moore. Ah! Mooré is open from 7:00 a.m. to 3:00 p.m. and serves specialty coffees such as "Lions Pride," along with espresso drinks, muffins, cakes, and pastries. Ah! Mooré is located in the southeast corner of the upper concourse (Level 2), at the top of the escalators from Gate G.

Ford Field also plays host to downtown Detroit's lunch crowd, with Adams St. concession stands "StrEATS of Detroit" and "No. 20's Pizza," open daily from 10:00 a.m. to 2:00 p.m.

Wayne County

Ford Field

Cost: 1-hour tours: adults $5; children and seniors $3.

For ticket information, call TicketMaster at (248) 645-6666, or see www.ticketmaster.com.

Directions: Exit I-75 at Warren Avenue, left on Woodward Avenue.

The Detroit Lions team store, the Roar & More, is open to the public from 10:30 a.m. to 3:00 p.m., giving fans a chance to check out all of the newest Lions merchandise on a daily basis.

For a more in-depth look at Ford Field, or if you don't think your kids can sit through an entire football game, the stadium offers one-hour behind-the-scenes tours. Tours begin in the Roar & More and feature luxury suites, the Detroit Lions' locker room, the team's new playing field and a look at the history of the area on which Ford Field stands. Two walk-up tours are available on a daily basis Monday through Friday, one beginning at 11:00 a.m. and one at 1:00 p.m., with a twenty-five-person capacity per tour. Tickets may be purchased at the Ford Field ticket windows inside the main entrance area or in the Ticket Office on Level 2. Group tours of twenty-five or more may be scheduled by calling (313) 262-2000.

Comerica Park (home of the Detroit Tigers)

2100 Woodward Avenue
Detroit, MI 48201
(313) 962-4000
www.detroittigers.com

If ever a professional sports venue resembled Disney World, this is it. Home to the Detroit Tigers baseball club, this place will keep the kids entertained even if the game drags.

Comerica Park
Directions: Exit I-75 at Warren Avenue, left on Woodward Avenue.

The Big Cat Carousel features thirty hand-painted tigers and two chariots, for those who need a break from the game. The fifty-foot Fly Ball Ferris Wheel invites riders into twelve baseball-shaped carts and offers a spectacular view of Detroit's skyline at the top. And the musical, "dancing," 150-foot fountain backed by the outfield wall—set off when a Tiger scores—is a quite sight to see. Taking in the park is an event itself, even if you're not a huge baseball fan.

Chapter Two

Ford-Wyoming Drive-in Theater

10400 Ford Road
Dearborn, MI 48126
(313) 846-6910

Ford-Wyoming Drive-in Theater

Hours: Evening double features, year-round; check local papers for times.

Directions: Exit I-94 at Ford Road (#210B), right on Addison Street, left on McGraw Street, which turns into Ford Road.

Drive-in theaters are a rarity these days, and one this size is pretty hard to find anywhere. Ford-Wyoming is the largest drive-in complex in Michigan, with eight separate screens, each showing a different film nightly. On a good summer weekend, there will be more than 2,000 cars and between 5,000 and 8,000 people there. It's a great place for parents to see a film and not worry about the kids disturbing other patrons. Plus, the little ones can sleep in the backseat if they need to. During the colder months, the theater offers window heaters so you're not tempted to keep the motor running.

Northville's Historic Marquis Theatre

135 E. Main Street
Northville, MI 48167
(248) 349-8110
www.northvillemarquistheatre.com

Northville's Historic Marquis Theatre

Hours: Vary by performance, call ahead for more info.

Cost: $7.50 for everyone, no children under 3.

Directions: Exit I-696 at I-275 south, take the Northville exit (#167), right on 8 Mile Road, left on Griswold Street, right on Main Street.

This is a beautiful theater that focuses solely on productions by and for children. The Marquis Theatre, a historic Northville landmark, is a restored Victorian building with nearly eighty years of rich history and tradition. Originally built as an opera house, this elegantly designed venue later presented vaudeville, featuring some of the finest acts of its time. During this era, Charlie Chaplin and Mary Pickford were among the many stars who appeared on the Marquis Theatre stage.

These days, holiday plays and time-honored productions, like *The Velveteen Rabbit*, are featured on a Thursday-through-Sunday schedule, including matinees.

Wayne County

Michigan State Fairgrounds

1120 W. State Fair Avenue
Detroit, MI 48203
(313) 369-8250
www.michiganstatefair.net

Michigan State Fairgrounds
Directions: Exit I-696 at Woodward Avenue, head south, left on State Fair Avenue.

Sonya discovers that you're never too old to enjoy a carousel ride.
Photo by Heidi Rehak Lovy

Home to the nation's oldest State Fair (it was established in 1849), these grounds are open all year and host a variety of events, including dog and horse shows, agricultural exhibits, concerts, a circus, and antique shows. Held every fall, the Michigan State Fair has everything you'd expect from such a production: carnival rides and games, barns full of livestock, and more junk food than you can possibly imagine. However, there are some features here that are pretty unique and outstanding. A perfect example of this is the "Miracle of Life" live birthing tent. It is here that you can witness in person everything from cows to pigs to goats being born and chicks hatching. (In our experience, the parents in the tent were more freaked out than the kids!)

Chapter Two

The Parade Studio

9600 Mt. Elliott Street
Detroit, MI 48211
(313) 923-7400
www.theparade.org

The Parade Studio

Directions: Take 8 Mile Road east to Dequindre Street, turn right; Dequindre curves to the left and becomes Conant Street; follow Conant to McNichols and turn left; right on Mound Road, which curves to the left and becomes Mt. Elliott Street.

America's Thanksgiving Parade is a Detroit tradition. Photo courtesy of The Parade Studio

Stepping foot in the Parade Studio is like entering a creative dreamscape. All the floats for America's Thanksgiving Day Parade, one of the largest televised parades in the country, are constructed and stored in this enormous warehouse that used to be an auto assembly plant. Visitors can check out, up-close, floats featuring Mother Goose, Santa, the Grinch, and many others. It's easy to spend hours watching the artists at work building the newest floats from wood, steel, Styrofoam, chicken wire, paint, and other materials. Also check out the giant papier-mâché heads collection (might be scary for little ones) and hundreds of costumes worn by parade participants every year. While currently the Parade Studio tour is open only to parties of twenty or more, by spring 2004 an expanded tour program will begin for smaller groups and individuals.

The new Parade Company will increase in size significantly and feature arts and educational programming and classes, events, and workshops and will be available for parties. Personally, I think this is one of the coolest things to do in Detroit, whether you live in the area or not. The actual parade travels down Woodward Avenue every Thanksgiving morning. To get a less-crowded sneak peek at the floats, check out the night-before lineup outside the Parade Company along Mt. Elliott Street. The organization also coordinates the International Freedom Festival, a weeklong July Fourth celebration, culminating with a spectacular fireworks display over the Detroit River.

A Parent's Guide to
Southeastern Michigan

Wayne County

Arts and Scraps
17820 E. Warren Avenue
Detroit, MI 48224
(313) 640-4411
www.artsandscraps.org

Arts and Scraps

Hours: 11am–6pm,
Tues–Thurs; 11am–4pm, Sat

Directions: From I-94, exit at
Cadieux Road, exit #223,
turn right on Cadieux, left
on E. Warren Ave.

This cool hat was created with recycled stuff from Arts & Scraps. Photo by Howard Lovy

Some kids really love junk. What seems to be trash to adults often is the making of a masterpiece for a child. Arts and Scraps knows that all too well. This nonprofit recycling company offers the opportunity for your child to grab a paper bag and fill it with industrial scraps of foam, fabric, brightly-colored pieces of fabric, and much, much more, then create an interesting craft project from these treasures. Some favorite creations are puppets, hats, and collages. With more than 300 selections to choose from, there's no problem finding just the right supplies. They even offer some "predesigned" projects for less than fifty cents, which does little damage to your child's allowance and a lot for their creativity. This is also a fabulous place to hold birthday parties for young, creative kids. I love that they take materials that would otherwise be discarded (more than twenty-two tons annually) and turn them into fun for kids.

Chapter Two

Parking It

Maybury State Park

Just west of Northville, entrance on Eight Mile Road, six miles west of I-275.
(248) 349-8390

This is one of our favorite places in all of Southeastern Michigan to spend a balmy summer day with the kids, the bikes, and a picnic lunch. In 1975, the Michigan Department of Natural Resources opened Maybury State Park on a farm in the northwest corner of Wayne County. The idea was to preserve a "living farm" close to the city, so residents, especially children, who have never experienced the sights, sounds, and—yes—smells of a working farm would have the opportunity to do so nearby. The area consists of several barns where visitors get a close, hanging-on-the-fence view of chickens, pigs, cows, goats, sheep, horses, and other typical farm animals. There is also a display of old farming equipment, but the staff that actually works on the land uses newer plows and harvesters. Kids not only get to feed the animals but also can view newborn chicks, modern tractors rumbling along, and huge draft horses pulling a plow through fields of corn, oats, beans, and other typical Michigan crops.

Also within the 1,000-acre State Park are natural areas of meadow and forests with hiking trails and bike paths. There is a higher-difficulty mountain bike trail, but we like to pedal around the scenic paved trails that are just hilly enough for little ones to have to walk their bikes at some points. A park concessionaire runs a horse stable with eight miles of horse trails. During the winter, cross-country skiers take advantage of these trails, and rental equipment is available at the park.

Maybury State Park

Cost: Call for prices. There is a $4 per car Michigan State Park fee, or you can purchase a $20 yearly pass that allows access to all state parks in Michigan.

Hours: Cross-country ski equipment rental is available noon–6pm Mon–Fri, and 9am–6pm Sat–Sun.

Directions: Exit I-275 south at 8 Mile (#167), head west about 6 miles; main entrance is off 8 Mile just past Beck Road.

Wayne County

Belle Isle

E. Jefferson Avenue at E. Grand Blvd.
Detroit, MI 48207
(313) 852-4075

Belle Isle

Hours: Daily 6am–10pm.

Cost: Free.

Directions: Exit I-375 at Jefferson Avenue, head east. Entrance is at the corner of Jefferson and East Grand Blvd.

This 985-acre island can best be described as downtown Detroit's playground. Located about four miles east of the Renaissance Center, the island affords some of the best Detroit and Windsor skyline views around. In addition to an aquarium, a nature center, a golf course, numerous historic buildings, and a museum, Belle Isle has twenty-some picnic shelters and tons of grills and picnic tables. Covered with more than eight miles of paved roads, its raceway has been the site of the mid-June Detroit Grand Prix. Frederick Law Olmstead designed the park, as well as the island's zoo, aquarium, and nature center. (He also designed New York's Central Park and the New Orleans City Park.) The island is also home to more than 120 beautiful European Fallow deer, and we're always quite amazed at how friendly they are. Sometimes they'll come right up to the car window looking for treats. Although this is a fantastic place to hang out with the family during the day, it tends to turn into a party place for older teens and adults at night. Stick to daylight hours.

The Dossin Great Lakes Museum, (313) 852-4051, features interesting models and great views of passing vessels during the summer shipping season.

Chandler Park Family Aquatic Center

12600 Chandler Park Drive
Detroit, MI 48224
(313) 822-7665

Chandler Park Family Aquatic Center

Hours: Open during the summer, though the end of August.

Cost: Ranges in price from $5 to $12, depending on age and day of the week.

Directions: Exit I-94 east at Conner Avenue (#220B), take Conner to Chandler Park Drive, turn left.

Cool off with the kids at Detroit's one and only water park—featuring a 4,800-square-foot play area for smaller kids dubbed the Tadpole Pool, a 203-foot Splash Down water slide, the Way Cool Wave Pool, and a Body Slide. Children must be forty-eight inches in height to ride water slides.

Chapter Two

Edward Hines Park

Edward Hines Drive, from Dearborn Heights to Northville
Westland, MI
(734) 261-1990
www.waynecounty.com/parks

> **Edward Hines Park**
>
> Directions: One of the many main entrances is at Edward Hines Drive and Merriman Road, 2 1/2 miles south of I-96. Park spans from Dearborn Heights to Northville.

This sixteen-mile-long park offers picnic areas, swings, slides, softball diamonds, and three manmade lakes (for canoeing and paddle boating, not swimming). From summer to fall, a portion of the park is closed to vehicles, and only bicycles and other nonmotorized vehicles are allowed during Saturdays and Sundays "In the Park." If you miss the weekend, try the bicycle trail anytime, which covers the entire length of the park. Near Nankin Mills in Westland, summer activities include outdoor movies and concerts. The park exists as a flood basin of the Middle Rouge River, and Edward Hines Drive winds along the river from Dearborn in the east to Northville in the west. In the winter, the park hosts Wayne County's annual LightFest, one of the best holiday displays in the Midwest, as well as trails for cross-country skiing and sled hills.

For Inquisitive Minds

The Charles H. Wright Museum of African American History, the Detroit Institute of Arts, and the New Detroit Science Center are all located within walking distance of each other near the south end of Detroit's Cultural Center. While all three may be a tad much to do in one day, if there are specific exhibits you're interested in, it's a nice stroll between each on a nice day.

Wayne County

Charles H. Wright Museum of African American History

315 E. Warren Avenue
Detroit, MI 48201
(313) 494-5800
www.maah-detroit.org

Detroit's African American roots run deep, and this amazing museum celebrates the rich tradition of the people, history, and culture through unique displays, including a life-size sculpture of the inside of a slave ship. On its face appear 2,500 names of ships that carried Africans across the Atlantic to the Americas as part of its core exhibit, *Of the People: The African American Experience*. The museum sponsors interactive exhibits, tours, and special events for families and children. Permanent exhibits trace the diverse history of African Americans to the present day, including the space suit worn by Mae Jemison, the first African American woman to fly on the space shuttle. Visitors will also learn about the Underground Railroad, the series of safe houses through which escaped slaves fled the South to freedom in the North before the Civil War.

> **Charles H. Wright Museum of African American History**
>
> Parking lot adjacent.
>
> Hours: 9:30am–5pm, Wed–Sat; 1–5pm, Sun.
>
> Cost: Adults $5; children 17 and under $3.
>
> Directions: Exit I-75 at Warren Avenue, head west.

Life-size sculpture. Courtesy of the Charles H. Wright Museum of African American History

Chapter Two

Detroit Institute of Arts

5200 Woodward Avenue
Detroit, MI 48202
(313) 833-7900
www.dia.org

Detroit Institute of Arts

Hours: 10am–4pm, Wed–Thurs;
10am–9pm, Fri; 10am–5pm, Sat–Sun.

Cost: Recommended donation:
adults $4, children $1

Directions: Exit I-75 at Warren
Avenue, head west, right on
Woodward Avenue.

The Detroit Institute of Arts (DIA) offers a remarkable range of mind-expanding activities, from children's and family workshops, youth and adult classes, and artists' demonstrations to special exhibitions, gallery talks, and more.

Walking around the museum itself might not hold the interest of kids, unless they're really into specific periods of art. But the DIA's Friday evening programs are sure to find the inner artist in the entire family. Family-friendly tours of specific galleries, jugglers, storytellers, live music, and crafts projects are just a few of the interesting things offered during these Friday events. One of the coolest things we've done during our several visits is participate in the pencil drawing tutorials. Local art school students were paired up with my stepdaughters in one of the Italian art galleries. They helped them choose a work they were particularly interested in and then coached them through creating their own version of it through pencil drawing.

The DIA offers hands-on arts and crafts workshops for families. Photo courtesy of the DIA

Also, for a nice, calm way to start your Sunday, try the DIA's Brunch with Bach series, which combines classical music and culinary artistry within the museum. It's held once a month on a Sunday. Call, or check the website for details.

Wayne County

The New Detroit Science Center

5020 John R Road
Detroit, MI 48202
(313) 577-8400
www.sciencedetroit.org

The New Detroit Science Center. Photo courtesy of the New Detroit Science Center

This is honestly one of those spots that will turn even the most uptight adult into a kid again, if only for a few hours; I've seen it firsthand. The Science Center was completely revamped in 2001, and now you'll find more than 110,000 square feet of hands-on exhibits, interactive theater performances, and some really cool films. Some of the exhibits in the motion and life sciences laboratories are reminiscent of something you might have found in Dr. Seuss's "Whoville," and personally, I could hang out here for hours. The layout is very kid-friendly, with lots of places to sit and plenty of easy-to-find restrooms. There's even a small café for those who just can't wait for a snack. One small warning: the IMAX Dome Theatre can be a little intimidating to some kids; be sure to prepare them for what's in store.

The New Detroit Science Center

Hours: 9am–3pm, Mon–Fri; 10:30am–6pm, Sat; noon–6pm, Sun.

Cost: Adults $7; seniors and kids 12 and under $6; children 2 and under, free. Entrance to IMAX Dome Theatre and planetarium $4 per person with general admission ticket.

Directions: Exit I-75 at Warren Avenue, head west, right on Woodward Avenue, right on Putnam Street, slight right on John R. Road.

Chapter Two

The Henry Ford,
America's Greatest History Attraction

20900 Oakwood Blvd.
Dearborn, MI
(313) 982-6100
www.hfmgv.org

It makes sense that the world's most complete collection of the history of transportation would be located in the Motor City. From the silly (a circa-1952 Oscar Mayer Wienermobile) to the somber (the presidential limo in which John F. Kennedy was assassinated), that's precisely what you'll find at The Henry Ford, America's Greatest History Attraction.

The ten-acre attraction, which includes Henry Ford Museum, Greenfield Village, and an IMAX theatre can seem intimidating in size alone, but the proof of human resourcefulness and ingenuity is sure to impress the entire family. For every item you instantly recognize, like a 600-ton steam-powered locomotive, there are 100 others that will make you stop and say "What the heck is THAT?"—like a sealed test tube that is said to hold Thomas Edison's last breath.

The older your kids are, the more you run the risk of hearing them bemoan the period-costume-clad staff who make candles and churn butter in the eighty-some acre Greenfield Village. But even the most cynical teenager will likely be impressed with Thomas Edison's Menlo Park, N.J., complex, which saw the invention of the phonograph and the incandescent light, and is reconstructed in the village. If all else fails, there's always the eye-popping imagery and booming sound of the jumbo IMAX Theatre to win them over.

The village offers special weekend exhibits and festivities, including horse-drawn carriage rides in warmer weather and fabulous sleigh rides in winter.

> **The Henry Ford, America's Greatest History Attraction**
>
> Hours: 9am–5pm, Mon–Sat; noon–5pm, Sun.
>
> Cost: Tickets for both museum and village: children under 12, $14; adults $20; separate tickets may be purchased for either the museum or the village. IMAX Theatre tickets are separate. Call for show listings.
>
> Directions: Exit the Southfield Freeway at the Rotunda Drive exit (#5), turn right on Rotunda, turn right on Oakwood Boulevard.

Entering Greenfield Village is like traveling back in time.
Photo courtesy of the Detroit Metro Convention and Visitors Bureau

Wayne County

Pewabic Pottery

10125 E. Jefferson Avenue
Detroit, MI 48214
(313) 822-0954
www.pewabic.com

Founded in 1903 during the height of the Arts and Crafts Movement, Pewabic Pottery was part of a trend that counteracted the regimented quality of products being produced by the Industrial Revolution. Even today, Pewabic Pottery stands as a testament to the beauty of pottery products in all their forms, from functional art to jewelry and tile, when they are crafted by hand. Designated as a National Historic Landmark, the house on Jefferson Avenue where Pewabic started now acts as a gallery for the works of chosen pottery artists from across the country, as well as a working studio that hosts workshops, lectures, and residency programs.

Most of the well-known potters from Michigan have taken a turn at the wheel here at one time or another. The pottery got its odd name from founder Mary Stratton, who took it from the name of a mine near the town where she grew up. Stratton apparently thought the Native American word referred to a type of clay, but it actually means "metal," or "steel." No matter, the name Pewabic now has another meaning. Along with an amazing gift shop and gallery, you can tour the behind-the-scenes working part of the studio. Also, choose from a variety of unique classes for kids and parents, many of which give you the opportunity to design and make your very own Pewabic tile.

Chapter Two

Distinctly Detroit

The Giant Uniroyal Tire
I-94 in Allen Park

> **The Giant Uniroyal Tire**
>
> Directions: From Metro Airport, head west on I-94. The Giant Uniroyal Tire is on the south side of I-94 in Allen Park.

This eight-story, all-weather radial may bring to mind a monster truck on steroids (if you think of monster trucks at all). Built for the 1964 New York World's Fair, the tire was originally a Ferris wheel. After the fair, it was rolled over to the car capital of America and stationed at the Uniroyal plant on Jefferson Avenue, across from Belle Isle. It has been modified and moved several times over the years and now greets visitors who have flown into Metro Airport as they make their way to downtown via I-94. It's strictly something to admire as you whiz by in the car. Its latest addition is a ten-foot-long nail embedded in the tire to promote a "self-healing" Tiger Paw nail guard.

Joe Louis Fist Sculpture
Woodward and Jefferson Avenues

> **Joe Louis Fist Sculpture**
>
> Directions: Exit I-375 at Jefferson Avenue west. The sculpture is at the intersection of Woodward and Jefferson Avenues.

When *The Fist*, as it's known, was unveiled, there was an uproar. You either love the sculpture or you hate it. It was during the height of Detroit's years as the murder capital that the Joe Louis fist was unveiled at the corner of Woodward and Jefferson Avenues. The impressive forearm of boxer Joe Louis encapsulated in bronze punches the air. As a monument to one of the most important sports figures to come out of Detroit, the structure is not only important but truly unique. It's located smack in the middle of one of the city's busiest intersections, so your view may only be possible from the car.

Wayne County

American and Lafayette Coney Islands

American: 114 W. Lafayette, Detroit (313) 961-7758
Lafayette: 118 W. Lafayette, Detroit (313) 964-8198

These next-door-neighbor eateries were opened by brothers who continue to battle it out over who has the best Coney dog. Located where Lafayette and Michigan Avenues merge, it's an easy jaunt after attending a game at Ford Field or Comerica Park. Both places are open twenty-four hours and feature the Motor City's version of Coney dogs—piled high with chopped onions, chili, and mustard—or loose burgers. Lafayette Coney Island features the waiters' trademark yelling of the customers' order to the kitchen. On nice days, the wait staff of both restaurants stand outside beckoning customers to one or the other. Which has the best food? You'll have to give them both a try and make that decision for yourself!

> **American and Lafayette Coney Islands**
>
> Directions: Exit I-75 at Warren Avenue, head west, left on Woodward Avenue, right on Lafayette.

Hockeytown Cafe

2301 Woodward Avenue
Detroit, MI 48201
(313) 965-9500

There should definitely be a serious sports fan in your party if you decide to dine here. But even kids without a lot of hockey knowledge may be amused by the gigantic hockey puck on the roof and ring of ice around the bar. This is more than a theme restaurant: This is a shrine to the Detroit Red Wings; remember, Detroit breeds serious hockey fans. Uniforms, photos, equipment, computer hockey trivia—the place is wall-to-wall shtick. Life-size sculptures of hockey greats, a 1962 model Zamboni, a "Walk of Fame," and other displays are enough to teach the novice everything about hockey. And the fun with hockey carries over to the menu: Find appetizers under the "pregame" heading and desserts in the "overtime" section.

> **Hockeytown Cafe**
>
> Hours: 11am-9pm, Sun-Tues; 11am-2am, Wed-Sat.
>
> Directions: Exit I-75 at Warren Avenue, head west, left on Woodward Avenue.

Chapter Two

Motown Historical Museum

2648 W. Grand Blvd
Detroit, MI 48208
(313) 875-2264

The Motown sound was born here.
Photo by Susan Stewar

Motown Historical Museum
Hours: noon–5pm, Sun–Mon; 10am–5pm, Tues–Sat.
Cost: Adults, $6; children under 12, $3.
Directions: Exit I-75 at W. Grand Blvd, head west.
Private parking lot.

After the glory of the auto magnates faded, the city experienced another heyday thanks to Berry Gordy. When he built a studio in this building in 1961, and modestly called it "Hitsville U.S.A.," he created a tempest that spawned the likes of Stevie Wonder, the Temptations, the Supremes, and many others. The studio-cum-museum is filled with some of the legends' old personal items. Kids into music will dig this place, but little ones might fast become bored. Luckily, it's small and doesn't take too long to absorb all the cool stuff.

Automotive Hall of Fame

21400 Oakwood Blvd
Dearborn, MI 48124
Adjacent to the Henry Ford,
America's Greatest History Attraction
(313) 240-4000
www.automotivehalloffame.org

The Hall of Fame honors greats in just about every aspect of the auto industry that you can imagine. And it really is more exciting than it sounds. In mockups of the inventors' workshops, kids can push buttons and hear portrayals of industry greats. Through hands-on displays, kids can learn how pioneers like Benz, Chevrolet, Chrysler, and Mack lent their names to their vehicles. The Hall of Fame also pays homage to pioneers who led the fight for worker rights in the 1930s, including a depiction of the West

Learn about the names behind the cars at the Automotive Hall of Fame. Photo courtesy of the Automotive Hall of Fame

Wayne County

Automotive Hall of Fame

Hours: Memorial Day through Oct. 31, 10am–5pm, 7 days a week; November through Memorial Day,10am–5pm, Tues–Sun.

Cost: Adults, $6; seniors $5.50; kids under 12 $3.

Directions: Exit the Southfield Freeway at the Rotunda Drive exit (#5), turn right on Rotunda, turn right on Oakwood Blvd.

Virginia kitchen where United Auto Workers leader Walter Reuther grew up, and the workshop of Ransom Olds that became the birthplace of mass production. There's also a lobby gift shop and a café with light refreshments.

Spirit of Detroit

Northeast corner of the Jefferson and Woodward Avenues intersection

Standing guard in front of the Coleman A. Young Building in bustling downtown Detroit is the twenty-six-foot sculpture the *Spirit of Detroit*. The piece, designed by Michigan sculptor Marshall Fredericks (1908–1998) in 1958, has been known to

Spirit of Detroit

Directions: Exit I-375 at Jefferson Avenue, head west. The Spirit of Detroit is located at the northeast corner of the Jefferson and Woodward Avenue intersection.

literally get into the spirit of things during major Motor City events. When the Red Wings win the Stanley Cup, a custom-made hockey jersey is draped over his body. When the Three Tenors performed here in 1999, he donned a spiffy custom-made tuxedo. Some think the custom is ridiculous, but many find it to be a wonderful reflection of the true spirit of Detroit.

Chapter Two

The People Mover

Stations in Greektown, the Renaissance Center,
Cobo Center and ten other locations
(313) 962-RAIL
www.ThePeopleMover.com

The People Mover

Hours: 7am–11pm, Mon–Thurs,
until midnight Fri–Sat,
and until 8pm, Sun.

Cost: 50 cents per person, per
ride; required tokens are
available at all stops.

A spin around town on Detroit's Central Automated Transit System definitely ranks high above any other tour of the city streets. Better known as the People Mover, the mass transit project was opened in 1987 after several years of delays and cost overruns. Some locals say the "train to nowhere" was purposely limited in its practicality to keep folks planted firmly in their driver's seats, but the ride is a great downtown primer. The 2.9-mile elevated track circles the heart of Detroit, connecting shopping centers, sports arenas, and the theater district. Its noticeably graffiti-less automated cars stop at thirteen stations, each decorated with beautiful mosaics, neon light sculptures, and other artwork.

The People Mover affords great views of Detroit and Windsor.
Photo courtesy of the Detroit Metro Convention and Visitors Bureau

The ride costs only fifty cents and lasts just fourteen minutes, but it gives an excellent overall view of the city from a superb, safe vantage point. First-time riders of all ages are sure to "ooh" and "ahh" a bit at the stretch when cars wind around Cobo Center and passengers see a panorama of the Detroit River and the skyline of Windsor, the Canadian city to the south.

A Parent's Guide to
Southeastern Michigan

Chapter Three

Oakland County

Named in the early 1800s for its abundance of beautiful oak trees, Oakland County boasts thirty downtown areas and many scenic, natural settings. Countless outdoor recreation opportunities are available, including three ski areas, twenty-seven public fishing sites, and more than sixty public golf courses. From hip, walkable downtowns to lush, wooded parks with lakes, the 873-square-mile Oakland County offers families practically every activity imaginable.

The 2000 U.S. Census reported 1.2 million people living in Oakland County—that's more than the entire state of Wyoming. Of those, about 83 percent are Caucasian, 10 percent are African American, and 4 percent are Asian. Between 1990 and 1999, the number of Oakland County households grew 14 percent to a total of 459,300, while the state of Michigan grew 6.1 percent. This becomes evident when driving through some of the northern cities and townships—there are new subdivisions sprouting up seemingly every year. More than two billion dollars were invested in construction projects in the county during 2000.

There are more natural lakes here than in any other county in the state. Oakland contains about 1,468 lakes and the headwaters of five major rivers: the Clinton, Huron, Rouge, Shiawassee, and Flint rivers. There are about 89,000 acres of public parks to roam about here, too. Oakland County is home to fourteen of Michigan's twenty-seven institutions of higher learning, including Lawrence Technological University and Oakland University. Top employers in Oakland County are General Motors, DaimlerChrysler, and William Beaumont Hospital.

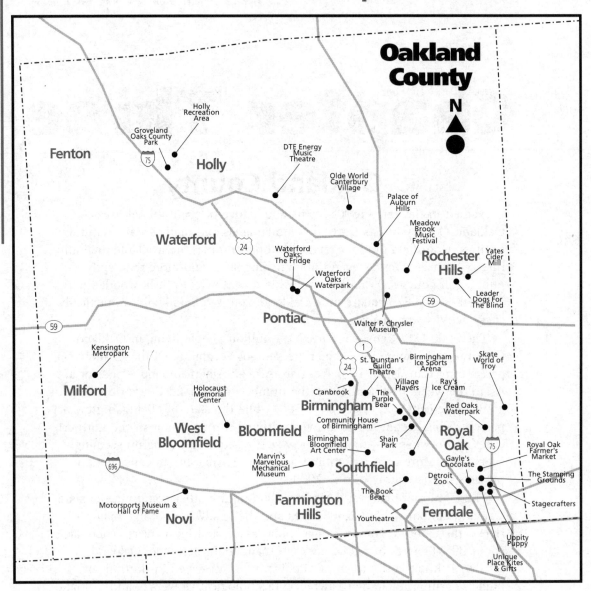

Oakland County

N ▲ ●

Fenton

Holly Recreation Area

Groveland Oaks County Park

75

Holly

DTE Energy Music Theatre

Olde World Canterbury Village

Palace of Auburn Hills

Meadow Brook Music Festival

Waterford

24

Waterford Oaks: The Fridge

Waterford Oaks Waterpark

Rochester Hills

Yates Cider Mill

Leader Dogs For The Blind

59

59

Pontiac

Walter P. Chrysler Museum

Kensington Metropark

1

24

St. Dunstan's Guild Theatre

Birmingham Ice Sports Arena

Skate World of Troy

Milford

Holocaust Memorial Center

Cranbrook

The Purple Bear

Village Players

Ray's Ice Cream

Birmingham

Red Oaks Waterpark

West Bloomfield

Bloomfield

Community House of Birmingham

Shain Park

Royal Oak

75

Royal Oak Farmer's Market

Marvin's Marvelous Mechanical Museum

Birmingham Bloomfield Art Center

Southfield

Gayle's Chocolate

The Stamping Grounds

696

Detroit Zoo

Motorsports Museum & Hall of Fame

Novi

Farmington Hills

The Book Beat

Youtheatre

Ferndale

Stagecrafters

Uppity Puppy

Unique Place Kites & Gifts

Oakland County

Just for Fun

Detroit Zoo

8450 W. 10 Mile Road
Royal Oak, MI 48067
(248) 398-0903
www.detroitzoo.org

Check out swimming polar bears at the Detroit Zoo's Artic Ring of Life exhibit. Photo courtesy of the Detroit Zoo

We live within walking distance of the Detroit Zoo, so it's high on our list of enjoyable things to do all year. It's clean, designed well, and easy to maneuver through with kids. Make sure to bring a camera, as photo opportunities abound.

This 125-acre park opened in 1928, the first in the United States to use barless exhibits, place animals in settings as close to their natural environment as possible, and confine them using dry or water moats for an unobstructed view.

Chapter Three

One of the newest exhibits, the Arctic Ring of Life, sprawls over 4.2 acres. Polar bears, Arctic foxes, snowy owls and harbor seals will become amicable roommates, or so you'll think. Thanks to a seventy-foot clear tunnel, you'll witness polar bears and seals frolicking in some 300,000 gallons of frigid salt water. In actuality, these two creatures aren't exactly compatible, but thanks to the genius of a unique ice acrylic barrier that actually separates them, it appears that they're one big, happy family.

Detroit Zoo

Cost: adults (13-61) $8; children (2-12) $6; seniors (62 and older) $6; free for children 2 and under.

Hours: 10am–4pm daily (Nov 1–Mar 31); 10am–5pm daily (Apr 1–Oct 31); closed Thanksgiving Day, Christmas Day, and New Year's Day.

Directions: Exit I-696 at Woodward Avenue, head north.

Another of the zoo's most popular features isn't an animal at all—it's the miniature railroad. If you hit every exhibit on your way to the back of the zoo, it's a nice break for tired feet to take the train back to the front.

Other popular attractions include the bear dens; the Holden Museum of Living Reptiles and Amphibians; the snow monkeys' hot-tub antics in the winter; the Chimps of Harambee, where you can view chimps in forest and meadow settings; and the Penguinarium, with its underwater views of the flightless birds.

Food here is limited to that of deep fried and junk food–type concessions; so pack a picnic lunch to enjoy in a large wooded grove near the front of the zoo.

The Detroit Zoo water tower is a familiar sight to anyone who travels local expressways.
Photo courtesy of the Detroit Zoo

Oakland County

Downtown Royal Oak

A prime spot for window-shopping, people-watching, or strolling, Royal Oak is an eclectic, cosmopolitan shopping, dining, and entertainment district. You'll find everything from retro-kitsch collectibles and trendy clothes for all ages, to great art and home furnishings. It's the perfect place to power shop for unique gifts or just browse the many galleries and antique shops. There is something interesting for kids on just about every block, and you won't have to worry about anyone going hungry with the variety of eateries spilling out onto the sidewalks of the downtown area. Teens will feel right at home in any of the numerous coffee shops and sidewalk cafes—it has long been a hangout for that age group during summer evenings. Most of walkable downtown Royal Oak is located between Lincoln and 11 Mile Road, and Lafayette Boulevard and Troy Street, about eleven miles north of Detroit.

> **Downtown Royal Oak**
>
> Directions: Exit I-696 at Main Street, head north on Main.

Gayle's Chocolates

417 S. Washington
Royal Oak, MI 48067
(248) 398-0001

As you enter Gayle's, the scent alone is enough to make you think you've entered some sort of decadent, treat-lovers' Valhalla. The artistic showcase of hand-dipped truffles, chocolate, and other candy concoctions are all made upstairs. The walls are lined with bins bursting with gourmet bulk candy. Adults are easily pleased, too, with potent, expertly made coffee drinks and fresh wheat grass shots that'll provide enough produce for your weekly allotment in one serving.

> **Gayle's Chocolates**
>
> Hours: 10am–6pm, Mon–Tues; 10am–11pm, Wed–Thurs; noon–6pm, Fri–Sat; closed Sunday
>
> Directions: Exit I-696 at Woodward Avenue/Main Street, head north on Woodward briefly, then bear right on Washington.

Chapter Three

BD's Mongolian Barbecue

310 S. Main Street
Royal Oak, MI 48067
(248) 398-7755
www.bdsmongolianbarbeque.com

> **BD's Mongolian Barbecue**
>
> Hours: 11am–11pm, Mon–Thurs;
> 11am–midnight, Fri–Sat;
> 11am–10pm, Sun.
>
> Directions: Exit I-696 at
> Woodward Avenue/Main
> Street, head north on Main.

This is the kind of restaurant that makes lunch or dinner more of an event than a meal. Older kids will "dig" rolling up their sleeves and creating their own stir-fry with a variety of meat, vegetables, sauces, and spices. Smaller kids will need some help. Recipe cards are provided for anyone who may not be a culinary whiz. But most everyone will enjoy watching the cooks prepare your creation, Mongolian style, on a huge open grill with long, stick-like cooking utensils.

Comet Burger

207 S. Main Street
Royal Oak, MI 48067
(248) 414-4567

> **Comet Burger**
>
> Hours: 11am–3am, Thurs–Sat;
> 11am–midnight, Sun–Wed.
>
> Directions: Exit I-696 at
> Woodward Avenue/Main
> Street, head north on Main.

You don't have to be a product of the 1950s to enjoy throwing down a chocolate malted shake or a few sliders amid pink vinyl-topped stools and Formica tables. Play some Elvis, wax nostalgic, and order a Philly steak for yourself. You can order a Sander's hot fudge cream puff (an over-the-top dessert with gobs of whipped cream) for the children.

Royal Oak Farmer's Market

316 E. 11 Mile Road
Royal Oak, MI 48067
(248) 548-8822

> **Royal Oak Farmer's Market**
>
> Hours: 7am–1pm, Sat, year-round; flea market
> 8am–3pm, every Sun.
>
> Directions: Exit I-696 at
> Woodward Avenue/Main
> Street, head north on Main,
> right on 11 Mile Road.

We think it's important for kids who grow up in urban or suburban settings to be aware of where their food comes from, and a trip to a local farmer's market brings them a bit closer than the usual grocery store stop. At the Royal Oak Farmer's Market, more than forty farmers, greenhouse producers, and crafters sell their products. Fresh cheese, organic produce, bread, and spices can also be found on most Saturdays.

Oakland County

Unique Place Kites and Gifts

525 S. Washington Avenue
Royal Oak, MI 48067
(248) 398-5900

This is one of those great, old toy stores that's packed from floor to ceiling with unusual stuff. Here you'll find a huge assortment of imported toys, the highly sought-after Beanie Babies, and you won't find a better variety of kites in the state.

Unique Place Kites and Gifts
Hours: 10:30am–6pm, Tues–Fri; 10:30am–5pm, Sat.
Directions: Exit I-696 at Woodward Avenue/Main Street, head north on Woodward briefly, then bear right on Washington, head north.

The Stamping Grounds

228 W. Fourth Street
Royal Oak, MI 48067
(248) 543-2190
www.stampinggrounds.com

Brimming with creative inspiration for you and your kids, the Stamping Grounds offers some interesting classes including card-making, tile-making, and more.

The Stamping Grounds
Hours: 11am–5pm, Tues–Wed; 11am–7pm, Thurs; 11am–5pm, Fri–Sat; closed Sun–Mon.
Directions: Exit I-696 at Main Street, head north on Main, left on Fourth Street.

The Uppity Puppy

706 S. Washington Avenue
Royal Oak, MI 48067
(248) 336-2380

If you love dogs, you have to at least browse here. Products range from the practical, like dog carriers and leashes, to the borderline absurd, like designer clothes and organic birthday cakes for your pooch.

The Uppity Puppy
Hours: 11am–7pm, Tues–Sat; 11am–3pm, Sun.
Directions: Exit I-696 at Woodward Avenue, head north on Woodward briefly, then bear right on Washington.

Stagecrafters

415 S. Lafayette Avenue
Royal Oak, MI 48067
(248) 541-6430
www.stagecrafters.org

Stagecrafters
Directions: Exit I-696 at Woodward Avenue/Main Street, head north on Woodward briefly, then bear right on Washington, head north, left on Fourth Street, left on Lafayette.
Cost: Ticket prices vary by performance.

Located in the historic Baldwin Theatre, the highly regarded troupe has two stages for live productions; a youth theater and a theater organ series. Kids' productions in the past have included *Pippi Longstocking* and *A Christmas Story*.

Chapter Three

Downtown Birmingham

With its designer boutiques, hip restaurants, and pampering spas, downtown Birmingham is Detroit's version of Beverly Hills. You'll find limitless gift shops, upscale toy stores, and galleries galore. This is a vibrant, pedestrian-friendly downtown that can either be a destination for families to take care of errands or for pure entertainment.

Community House of Birmingham

380 S. Bates Street
Birmingham, MI 48009
(248) 644-5832
www.communityhouse.com

Offers educational programs for all ages, an early childhood center, antiques festival, art show, and music programs, just to name a few.

Community House of Birmingham

Directions: Exit I-696 at Woodward Avenue, head north about 4 1/2 miles, bear left on Old Woodward Avenue into downtown Birmingham, left on Frank Street, right on Bates.

Shain Park

One square block bordered by
Henrietta, Martin, Bates,
and Merrill Streets
Birmingham, MI 48009

This park reminds me of an old-fashioned town square in a city that strives to simultaneously be cutting edge and small town. An extraordinary sculpture by Marshall Fredericks is at the center of this park, itself the core of a

Shain Park

Directions: Exit I-696 at Woodward Avenue, head north about 4 1/2 miles, bear left on Old Woodward Avenue into downtown Birmingham, left on Frank Street, right on Bates.

downtown area (one of the few) that can still attract enough shoppers to keep both chain stores and high-end boutiques in business. Shain Park plays host to a plethora of city events, such as New Year's Eve fireworks and an ice show in the winter, numerous concerts in the summer, and the last art fair of the season every September. Most weekdays, you'll find stay-at-home parents gathering here while their kids enjoy the playscape.

Oakland County

Birmingham Bloomfield Art Center

1516 Cranbrook Road
Birmingham, MI 48009
(248) 644-0866
www.bbartcenter.org

The Birmingham Bloomfield Art Center (BBAC) serves all ages as an art school and community center for programs in the visual

Birmingham Bloomfield Art Center

Directions: Exit I-696 at Evergreen Road (#11), right on Evergreen, which turns into Cranbrook Road.

arts. Classes offered include calligraphy, painting, jewelry, sculpture, stained glass, and many others. Check out the special children's classes and workshops that parents and children can attend together. The BBAC is a nonprofit, member-supported organization that was founded in 1957 by a group of concerned citizens interested in providing cultural opportunities for the community.

The Purple Bear

244 E. Maple Road
Birmingham, MI 48009
(248) 645-0400

A great place to look for shower gifts, the Purple Bear offers beautiful (though a tad pricey) nursery bedding and décor, and clothing for infants and toddlers.

The Purple Bear

Hours: 10am–6pm daily

Directions: Exit I-696 at Woodward Avenue, head north, left on Maple Road.

Birmingham Ice Sports Arena

2300 E. Lincoln Street
Birmingham, MI 48009
(248) 645-0731

Enjoy indoor ice-skating during open skate hours (call ahead for times), skating lessons, and ice hockey groups.

Birmingham Ice Sports Arena

Directions: Exit I-696 at Woodward Avenue, head north, right on Adams Road, right on Lincoln Street.

Chapter Three

Village Players

752 Chestnut Street
Birmingham, MI 48009
(248) 644-2075
www.villageplayers.com

The Village Players in Birmingham celebrated its eightieth season in 2003 and boasts more than 225 members. Over the years, the group has taken on more than 400 productions and given more than 1,200 performances to local audiences at its prominent location on Chestnut Street, just off Woodward Avenue.

St. Dunstan's Guild Theatre

400 Lone Pine Court
Bloomfield Hills, MI 48304
(248) 644-0527
www.stdunstanstheatre.com

Each season includes six shows: four in the indoor playhouse and a production performed in the outdoor Cranbrook Greek Theatre each June. In November, they also present a Children's Theatre production.

The Palace of Auburn Hills

2 Championship Drive
Auburn Hills, MI 48326
(248) 377-0100
www.palacenet.com

The Palace of Auburn Hills. Photo by Mark Attard

This 20,000-plus-seat venue hosts a cornucopia of world-class sporting and entertainment events. The NBA's Detroit Pistons call The Palace home, but the arena also hosts special events and concerts throughout the year. The Backstreet Boys, Peter Gabriel, and U2 are among the live acts that have wowed audiences at

Oakland County

The Palace of Auburn Hills

Directions: Exit I-75 at Lapeer Road (#81), right on Lapeer Road, left on Championship Drive.

the Palace. There are plenty of food options here, too, from traditional arena concessions to higher-end sit-down restaurants. Tours of the facility are available by calling (248) 377-8278—this may be a lower-cost way to check out the luxury suites.

Meadow Brook Music Festival

3554 Walton Blvd
Oakland University
Rochester, MI 48309
(248) 377-0100
www.palacenet.com

Meadow Brook Music Festival

Directions: Exit I-75 at University Drive (#79), left on Squirrel Road, right on Walton Blvd.

Each year Meadow Brook hosts about forty shows in its outdoor amphitheater. The annual summer festival offers a variety of entertainment choices including pop, rock, country, jazz, folk music, and comedy and stage productions. Tucked in the woods on the far side of Oakland University's campus, Meadow Brook allows lawn-ticket holders to get up-close to performers, as the area wraps around the pavilion seating area. Smaller than its sister venue, DTE Energy Music Theatre, Meadow Brook is also the summer home to the Detroit Symphony Orchestra.

Meadow Brook Music Festival

Chapter Three

DTE Energy Music Theatre

7773 Pine Knob Road
Clarkston, MI 48348
(248) 377-0100
www.palacenet.com

DTE Energy Music Theatre

Directions: Exit I-75 at Sashabaw Road (#89), right on Sashabaw, right on Clarkston Road, right on Pine Knob Road.

DTE Energy Music Theatre

With its waterfalls, homey landscaping, and patron-friendly layout, the DTE has earned a reputation as one of the top venues in the nation. The DTE is clean, the parking lot is easily accessible, the security staff is on top of things and affable, and the concession stands offer more than the standard hot dogs and chips. There are often family-oriented productions held during the day in summer months.

Oakland County

Youtheatre

15600 J. L. Hudson Drive
Southfield, MI 48075
(248) 557-PLAY (7529)
www.youtheatre.org

Youtheatre programs are professional, educational theater performances for children, families, students, and teachers. Cool workshops are offered every Saturday between performances for $8 per child. Topics have included basic acting, stage movement, puppetry, and improvisation.

Ray's Ice Cream

4233 Coolidge Highway
Royal Oak, MI 48073
(888) 549-5256
www.raysicecream.com

For many local families, a trip to Ray's for a scoop is a highly anticipated summertime tradition. Despite its relatively modern exterior, Ray's is old-fashioned—not only because its soda fountain still looks the way it did when it was moved there from another location in 1958, but because it's one of only a handful of shops that actually still makes its own ice cream. Ray's is a true family business. The grandsons of original owner, Ray Stevens, still make the ice cream using a recipe that has been in the family for generations. You don't usually share secrets like that, but the owner will tell you one thing: the butterfat content of the ice cream made at Ray's is the highest in the state. Ray's still sells some 1950s favorites, like lemon ice cream, along with more current fare like Almond Joy. One of the biggest sellers, though, is a fad from the turn of the last century—ice cream molded into shapes like peaches, pears, and flowers that look startlingly like the real thing. The molds are mostly wholesaled to country clubs and hotels across the country, but you can order one for yourself by calling ahead. One word of warning: the ice cream at Ray's is a little pricey. They don't skimp on the servings, though, and one scoop is enough for many hearty appetites.

Chapter Three

Marvin's Marvelous Mechanical Museum

31005 Orchard Lake Road
Farmington Hills, MI 48334
(248) 626-5020
www.marvin3m.com

> **Marvin's Marvelous Mechanical Museum**
>
> Hours: 10am–10pm, Mon–Thurs, 10am–11pm, Fri–Sat, 11am–9pm, Sun.
>
> Cost: Free admission, but bring plenty of quarters—just about every machine and game here requires at least one.
>
> Directions: Exit I-696 at Orchard Lake Road, head north about 2 1/2 miles. Museum is on the left.

Before Game Cubes, kids enjoyed pinball. Before then, arcade parlors featured coin-operated plane rides and ancient fortune-telling machines. Truly a rare find, Marvin's Marvelous Mechanical Museum pays homage to all these coin-operated games. Marvin's houses an awe-inspiring range of toys and gadgets dating back to the early nineteenth century—it's a blast of nostalgia you might have a hard time topping anywhere else. Alas, Marvin provides current video games to keep modernist children happy, too.

Olde World Canterbury Village

2369 Joslyn Court
Lake Orion, MI 48360
(248) 391-5700 or (800) 442-XMAS
www.canterburyvillage.com

> **Olde World Canterbury Village**
>
> Hours: 10am–5:30pm daily, extended hours during holiday season
>
> Directions: Exit I-75 at Joslyn Road (#83), head north about 3 miles.

Olde World Canterbury Village

Originally a successful farm established by *Detroit Evening News* publisher William E. Scripps, Canterbury Village reopened in 1993 and sprawls across twenty-one acres. The Toy Store lures adults and children alike with a unique selection of merchandise and interactive displays. The Gift Store houses Boyds Bears, collectible steins, swords, cannon replicas, and an aromatic candle shop. The Always Christmas shop provides some 90,000 square feet of year-round holiday shopping. After browsing the shops, wander over to the Village Pavilion to see a gorgeous reproduction of a nineteenth-century German carousel that kids can take a spin on. Outside you'll find a matching Ferris wheel and train that operate seasonally.

Oakland County

Skate World of Troy

2825 Maple Road
Troy, MI 48083
(248) 689-4100

When the weather outside is frightful, as it so often is in Michigan, pack up the children, strap on some skates (either inline or roller), and get some exercise at Skate World. Call ahead to inquire about regularly scheduled special events and theme parties.

> **Skate World of Troy**
>
> Hours: vary by theme nights.
>
> Cost: Varies by theme nights.
>
> Directions: Exit I-696 at Dequindre Road (#20), head north about 5 miles, left on Maple Road.

Parking It

Dinosaur Hill Nature Preserve

33 North Hill Circle
Rochester, MI 48307
(248) 656-0999

Don't count on seeing T-Rex, but do count on observing the natural beauty of sixteen acres of meadows and woods that ramble alongside a picturesque stream. Families can view nature at its liveliest or view stuffed animals inside the learning center. If you're allergic to bees, steer clear of the productive beehive. The self-marked nature trails offer an exhilarating hike at anytime of the year.

> **Dinosaur Hill Nature Preserve**
>
> Hours: Open dawn–dusk
>
> Cost: No entry fee
>
> Directions: Exit I-75 at Rochester Road (#67), head north about 9 miles, left on Glendale Court, right on Oak Street, left on North Hill Circle.

Chapter Three

Waterford Oaks: The Fridge

1702 Scott Lake Road
Waterford, MI 48328
(248) 975-4440
www.co.oakland.mi.us/parksrec/ppark/fridge.html

The toboggan run at The Fridge has a fifty-five-foot drop. Photo courtesy of Oakland County Parks

Appropriately named, the Fridge offers a climate-controlled ultimate toboggan run. Unlike any other in Oakland or surrounding counties, the run is 1,000 feet long, with the first dip dropping fifty-five feet. The rest is like an icy-snow roller-coaster ride taking you up to speeds of thirty miles an hour, leaving riders wanting to do it over and over. The best part—besides the exhilarating thrill—is that toboggans are provided. After the run, warm up in front of the fireplace in the lodge with a steaming cup of hot cocoa. Check the website for cost-saving coupons.

Waterford Oaks: The Fridge

Hours: 4–9:30pm, Wed–Fri; 10am–10pm, Sat; noon–6pm, Sun.

Cost: Unlimited rides: adults $9 (residents $7); kids $4; or $2.50 per individual ride

Directions: Exit I-75 at Square Lake Road, head west, right on Telegraph Road, head north about 5 miles, right on Scott Lake Road.

Special rules: Must be at least 30" to ride, and children under 43" must be accompanied by an adult. Dress warm!

Oakland County

Waterford Oaks Waterpark

1702 Scott Lake Road
Waterford, MI 48328
(248) 858-0918

Cooling off at Waterford Oaks Waterpark. Photo courtesy of Oakland County Parks

Waterford Oaks Waterpark

Hours: Seasonally, 11am–7pm.

Cost: Varies, call or check website.

Directions: Exit I-75 at Square Lake Road, head west, right on Telegraph Road, head north about 5 miles, right on Scott Lake Road.

Kids can cool off in the "Big Bucket," a water playground featuring more than thirty interactive activities, and "Ragin' Rapids," a three-story raft ride that ends with a splash. Also at the park are a wave pool, water slides, and picnic areas. It's a nice option when you don't have time to drive to the beach.

Chapter Three

Red Oaks Waterpark

1455 E. 13 Mile Road
Madison Heights, MI 48328
(248) 858-0918

What stands out at this water park is the play area for toddlers, with water jets and other fun stuff for really little ones. All the usual water slides and wave pools are here, too.

Groveland Oaks County Park

14555 Dixie Highway
Holly, MI 48442
(248) 634-9811

Red Oaks Waterpark

Hours: 11am–7pm, seasonally.

Cost: Varies, call or check website.

Directions: Exit I-696 at Dequindre Road (#20), head north about 2 1/2 miles, left on 13 Mile Road.

Rent a boat and spend a day on the water at Groveland Oaks. Photo courtesy of Oakland County Parks

Groveland Oaks County Park

Hours: 8am–sunset.

Directions: Exit I-75 at Dixie Highway (#93), turn right, travel about 7 miles to the park.

This park boasts the largest playscape for kids in the Oakland County Parks system. It also offers bike and boat rentals, a spiral waterslide into Stewart Lake, and camping sites.

Oakland County

Yates Cider Mill

1990 Avon Road
Rochester, MI 48307
(248) 651-8300
www.yatescidermill.com

It's fun to spend a crisp, autumn day at Yates Cider Mill. Photo by Howard Lovy

Yates Cider Mill opened in 1863 as the Yates Grist Mill beside the waters of the Clinton-Kalamazoo Canal. By 1876 it was reborn as a cider producer and its name officially changed. Today you can visit the mill and it looks very much like it did way back when—only now you can tour the Mill, indulge in the cider, doughnuts, caramel apples, apple butter, apple pies, knackwurst, and hot dogs made on the premises. You can even bag your own apples from boxes picked from the orchard. In addition, the 1,200-acre park surrounding the Mill is open for enjoyment every fall not only for hiking, picnicking, and beautiful scenery, but also for pony rides and a petting farm. Don't forget to visit the fudge shop just over the bridge. Group tours are available.

Yates Cider Mill

Hours: Seven days in Sept–Oct, 9am–7pm; 7 days in Nov, 9am–5pm.

Directions: Exit I-75 at Exit #65A, turn right on 14 Mile Road, left on Dequindre, travel about 9 miles to Avon Road and turn right.

Chapter Three

Nature Center at George W. Suarez Friendship Woods

30300 Hales Street
Madison Heights, MI 48071
(248) 585-0100

Nature Center at George W. Suarez Friendship Woods

Hours: 10am–6pm, Tues; noon–8pm, Wed; 10am–6pm, Thurs; 10am–5pm, Fri; noon–5pm, Sat–Sun; closed Monday.

Directions: Exit I-696 at John R Road, head north, right on 13 Mile Road, right on Hales Street.

Just a short drive from what seems like an area of never-ending strip malls and shopping centers, it's nice to be able to seek reprieve in the woods. The Nature Center offers some interesting displays on local history and nature. There is a small gift shop and interesting programs are offered here, too. We actually handled some huge snakes and exotic frogs at an event they had. A simple paved trail leads you over a mile through rustic woods that makes you feel like you've driven up north, minus the hills. Birthday parties can be scheduled on Saturdays, for a fee, and those unable to walk the trails can take advantage of a special golf cart tour.

Independence Oaks

9501 Sashabaw Road
Clarkston, MI 48348
(248) 625-0877

Independence Oaks

Hours: 8am–sunset, daily

Cost: $8 per car; $5 for residents; $3 for seniors.

Directions: Exit I-75 at Sashabaw Road (#89), turn right. Park is less than 3 miles off the expressway.

Independence Oaks is just one of the many area parks open for cross-country skiing. Photo courtesy of Oakland County Parks

By the time you get this far north in Oakland County, it actually becomes a little hilly! At Independence Oaks, the ten miles of marked nature and ski trails are a delight—refreshingly more challenging than some other county parks in flatter terrains. Cyclists, runners, walkers, and bladers enjoy a 2.5-mile paved pathway through scenic woods. Families can rent canoes and paddleboats to traverse parts of the sixty-eight-acre Crooked Lake at a leisurely pace.

Oakland County

Boulan Community Park

West off Crooks Road, between Big Beaver and Wattles Roads
(248) 524-3484

This fifty-three-acre community park has three baseball diamonds, four tennis courts, a football field, two sand volleyball courts, three full-size soccer fields, two large play structures, picnic areas, and ample restrooms. In short, you will undoubtedly find something active for you and your kids to do here.

> **Boulan Community Park**
>
> Cost: Free.
>
> Directions: Exit I-75 at Big Beaver Road, head west, right on Crooks.

Holly Recreation Area

8100 Grange Hall Road
Holly, MI 48442
(248) 634-8811

What I find so fascinating about this park is that it's less than a one-hour drive away from downtown Detroit, and you can go camping. The area comprises about 8,000 acres, ranging from undeveloped natural areas of woods, fields, lakes, and marshes to thoroughly modern facilities for day use and campground areas. Families can relax away summer days swimming at two beaches, fishing hiking, camping, water-skiing, and picnicking. There are also some rather challenging mountain bike trails for the more adventurous.

> **Holly Recreation Area**
>
> Directions: Exit I-75 at Grange Hall Road (#101), right on Grange Hall Road about 1 mile.

Paint Creek Trail

4393 Collins Road
Rochester, MI 48306
(248) 651-9260

The Paint Creek Trail is the most beautiful when the leaves are changing to brilliant hues in the autumn. But the former railroad is rather scenic any time of the year—for walking, running, cross-country skiing, biking, and blading. The paved trail runs 8.5 miles between the city of Rochester and the village of Lake Orion.

> **Paint Creek Trail**
>
> Directions: Exit I-75 at Grange Hall Road (#101), right on Grange Hall.

Chapter Three

Kensington Metropark

2240 W. Bruno Road
Milford, MI 48380
(248) 685-1561

Enjoy a stroll at Kensington Metropark.
Photo courtesy of Huron-Clinton Metroparks

Kensington Metropark

Hours: 6am–10pm daily.

Cost: Vehicle entry permit required: Annual $20 (seniors $12); daily permit $4.

Directions: Exit I-96 at #153 and turn right directly into the park.

Picturesque Kent Lake is surrounded by the 4,357-acre Kensington Park, which allows outdoor enthusiasts a year round place for fun, sun, and winter recreation. Scenic hiking, biking, driving, and fitness trails are merely a sampling of the many things Kensington has to offer. For the avid boater, two launching ramps are available. Rental of paddleboats and rowboats provide water fun for everyone. The Island Queen, an excursion boat with capacity for sixty-six passengers, makes trips every hour during the summer (group charters also are available). For the more sporty, fishing and golfing are at your disposal. During the winter season, the park features cross-country skiing, an ice rink, tobogganing, and sledding. The general consensus is that if you can't find something to do here, you apparently aren't looking hard enough.

At night, part of the park can become a rowdy, party place for young adults; so unless you're there for a special event, you might want to pack up the kids around sunset.

Oakland County

Meininger Park

Corner of Maxwell and Farnum Streets
Royal Oak, MI 48067

We fondly refer to this park as "Dog Park," or even more abbreviated, "DP." It's our favorite local park. Hardly flashy, the city-run park is just about the length of two city blocks. It features two tennis courts and a nice playscape. What we love most about it is that it's a dog run. On most weekdays after 5:00 p.m. and anytime during the weekend there are gatherings of at least a few dozen dogs of all breeds frolicking among the heavily wooded park. For canine lovers of all ages, it's the perfect place to relax and get some fresh air.

Meininger Park

Hours: 6am–9pm.

Directions: Exit I-696 at Woodward Avenue, head north, right on 11 Mile Road, left on Maxwell.

For Inquisitive Minds

Cranbrook

39221 Woodward Avenue
Bloomfield Hills, MI 48303
(887) 462-7262
www.cranbrook.edu

A first-timer's arrival at Cranbrook is probably comparable to what Alice encountered in Wonderland. Lush, elaborate gardens lead you to hidden sculptures and reflection ponds. Your senses come alive viewing stunning Gothic, Tudor, and modern-style buildings that house historic sites and learning centers.

George Gough Booth, publisher of the *Detroit Evening News* (now the *Detroit News*), founded Cranbrook in the early 1900s as a home for his family and a learning facility. The 300-plus acre Cranbrook was designated a National Historic Landmark in 1989.

Cranbrook

Institute of Science:

Hours: 10am–5pm daily, until 10pm Fri.

Cost: Adults (13–64) $7; children (2–12) and seniors (65 and older) $5.

House and Gardens:

Hours: Guided tours for Cranbrook House and Gardens are available; call for dates and times; self-guided tours of Cranbrook Gardens are available daily, May through Labor Day, 10am–5pm.

Cost: Varies; call or see website for details.

Museum:

Hours: 11am–5pm, Tues–Sun; 11am–9pm, every fourth Fri.

Cost: Adults $5; students with ID $3; seniors (65 and older) $3; children 7and younger free.

Directions: Exit I-696 at Woodward Avenue, head north about 6 miles.

Chapter Three

Sculptures greet visitors to the Cranbrook Art Museum.
Photo by Howard Lovy

While part of the Cranbrook grounds includes a private school and an exclusive art academy, there are also plenty of educational opportunities for the general public at Cranbrook. If a giant T. Rex skeleton isn't enough to get you to visit the Cranbrook Institute of Science, go for the planetarium or the "Bat Zone," a permanent educational exhibit focusing on the winged creatures.

"This is the only place in Michigan where kids can interact elbow-to-elbow with working scientists," says Institute of Science Director Mike Stafford. "Their work is the basis for most of our exhibits, classes, and collections."

Oakland County

The author quickly exits the Bat Zone—home to many live bats!
Photo by Howard Lovy

Visitors can tour Cranbrook House and its surrounding gardens, too. World-renowned Detroit architect Albert Kahn designed the Booth family's Late Gothic Revival residence in 1917 and 1918. The forty acres of gardens are open May through October.

For Mom and Dad, or kids with an eye for the arts, the Cranbrook Art Museum is certain to wow. In its 100-year history, the museum has served as a staple not only to the community, but also to the art world as a whole. The permanent collection features work from influential artists like Frank Stella, Andy Warhol, and Jackson Pollack.

Chapter Three

Holocaust Memorial Center

6602 W. Maple Road
West Bloomfield, MI 48322
(248) 661-0840
www.holocaustcenter.org

Holocaust Memorial Center

Hours: 10am–4pm, Sun–Thur; 9am–1pm, Fri;
public guided tour, 1pm, every Sun & Wed.

Cost: Admission is free,
but donations are welcome.

Directions: Exit I-696 at Telegraph Road,
head north, left on Maple Road.

This is a solemn place to visit, there's no doubt about it. It may not be appropriate for really young children, but those a little older could learn something at the Holocaust Memorial Center. Visitors pass by an eerily beautiful Memorial Flame that burns for the six million Jews killed in the Holocaust; a small theater screens video of survivors recounting their experiences, and many other exhibits document the atrocity that was the Holocaust. The Center broke ground in 2002 for a new facility, several times the size of the existing structure. The new building, tentatively scheduled to open in late 2003, will be located at 28123 Orchard Lake Road, Farmington Hills.

Motorsports Museum & Hall of Fame

43700 Expo Center Drive
Novi, MI 48375
(800) 250-RACE
www.mshf.com

Motorsports Museum & Hall of Fame

Hours: 10am–5pm, daily in summer;
10am–5pm, Thurs–Fri in winter.

Cost: Adults $3;
kids under 12 and seniors $2.

Directions: Exit I-96 at Novi Road
(#162), left on Novi Road, right
on Fonda Street, right on
Expo Center Drive.

This compact museum, located at the base of the Novi Expo Center Water Tower, pays homage to all things motor sports-related. If you follow racing, a stop here is mandatory during a Detroit area visit.

Challenge your companions to a race on the four-lane slot car track, where scale model electric stock cars zoom around a track. Or climb into the coin-operated video simulation racecar that pits you against another driver.

Inside the main exhibit area, changing displays include more than thirty racing vehicles, from current Indy-style cars, stock cars, and drag strip models to turn-of-the-century vehicles, including motorcycles, power boats, and a racing airplane.

Kids can have their picture taken in the driver's seat of a real Winston Cup stock car. Four video screens play race footage throughout the display area while a gift shop supplies everything from collectible model cars to T-shirts and other souvenirs.

Oakland County

Walter P. Chrysler Museum

1 Chrysler Drive
Auburn Hills, MI 48326
(888) 456-1924
www.museum.chrysler.com

Walter P. Chrysler Museum

Hours: 10am–6pm, Tues–Sat; noon–6pm, Sun; closed Mon.

Cost: General admission $6; children (6–12) $3; seniors (65 and older) $3; children (5 and under) free.

Directions: Exit I-75 at Chrysler Drive (#78), continue on Chrysler Drive to the museum.

They don't call this the Motor City for nothing. The Chrysler Museum opened in 1999 on the grounds of DaimlerChrysler's enormous Auburn Hills complex. It's the first on-site museum built by a North American auto company.

Inside are life-size dioramas, interactive displays, a video wall, and timelines detailing the history of the car company that Walter Chrysler founded in 1924. But the main attraction here is the cars themselves—and this should help in determining if you should take the kids or not. Ask yourself, "Are they interested in cars?" If the answer is "no," it may not be a good idea.

Just inside the front door is a massive, seventy-five-foot stainless steel structure that holds aloft a 1941 Thunderbolt and a red 1989 Viper. It is called the Tower, which rotates to give visitors a complete view of the impressive cars. Other vehicles on exhibit include rare Rambler, DeSoto, and Hudson models, as well as concept cars and trucks.

The Book Beat

26010 Greenfield Road
Oak Park, MI 48237
(248) 968-1190

The Book Beat

Hours: 10am–9pm, Mon–Sat; 11am–6pm, Sun.

Directions: Exit I-696 at Greenfield Road (#13), head north.

This is one of the few, great independent bookstores left in Metro Detroit. The children's area has an outstanding variety for all ages, albeit a tad disorganized and chaotic at times, just like kids themselves. The knowledgeable staff will help you find just about anything you need. If they don't have it (which they probably do, and signed by the author to boot) they'll order it for you.

Chapter Three

Leader Dogs for the Blind

1039 S. Rochester Road
Rochester, MI 48308
(888) 777-5332
www.leaderdog.org

Since the Leader Dogs for the Blind headquarters is in Rochester, Mich., it's not uncommon to happen across a leader dog in training at area malls or just walking down the street. No matter how incredibly cute the dog or puppy is, don't try to pet him—he's hard at work.

Leader Dogs for the Blind

Hours: Call ahead to arrange for a tour of the facilities.

Directions: Exit I-75 at Rochester Road (#67), turn right, building is about 8 miles down Rochester Road.

Leader Dogs for the Blind was founded in 1939 by a group of Michigan Lions. Their goal was to train dogs to lead the blind and to provide facilities and means where trained dogs could be matched to a blind master. More than 10,000 blind people have become self-sufficient through the use of a Leader Dog—usually German Shepherds, Labradors, and Golden Retrievers.

The tour includes an inside look at how dogs are trained for such a huge responsibility.

Chapter Four

Macomb County

Whenever our family ventures east over to Macomb County, I've always been struck by how rural much of the area is—it has always been like spending a day in the country for us. But one thing has been happening over the past few years to change that: Development. Macomb County is home to some of the fastest growing communities in Michigan. In fact, for several years in a row the largest numbers of building permits in the state were issued in this county. New subdivisions are almost as prevalent now as are the wide-open terrain and wooded areas. But the charm and opportunities for recreation and entertainment have so far withstood the growth.

Macomb County is located in Southeastern Michigan along the western Lake St. Clair shoreline, adjacent to Metro Detroit to the south. There are approximately 788,000 residents in its 482 square miles. Of those, 93 percent are Caucasian and 3 percent are African American. It contains a diverse economy, strong in the area of auto-industry production. Top employers include General Motors, DaimlerChrysler, and Visteon. Its geographic diversity includes heavily populated urban areas to the south and an urbanized country-like setting to the north.

Choose your frustration from fourty-seven public golf courses or partake in the nautical. This is the freshwater boating capital of the world, with more registered pleasure boats than any other county in the United States. There are recreational harbor facilities at St. Clair Shores Metro Beach and Clinton River on Lake St. Clair. There are more than 6,500 acres of parks, including two Huron Metroparks here, too. Downtown Mount Clemens has a lot to offer in the way of coffee shops, restaurants, specialty stores, and quaint villages abound in Macomb County. Check out the Victorian charm of Romeo or the historical buildings of downtown Utica.

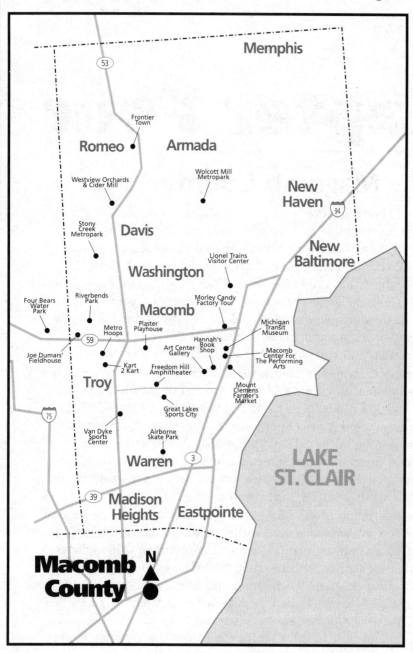

Memphis

53

Frontier
Town

Romeo   Armada

Westview Orchards
& Cider Mill   Wolcott Mill
Metropark   New
Haven   94

Stony
Creek
Metropark   Davis
New
Washington   Baltimore

Lionel Trains
Visitor Center

Four Bears   Riverbends   Macomb   Morley Candy
Water   Park   Factory Tour
Park   Michigan
Plaster   Transit
Metro   Playhouse   Museum
Hoops   Hannah's
59   Art Center   Book
Shop
Gallery
Joe Dumars'   Macomb
Fieldhouse   Kart   Center For
2 Kart   Freedom Hill   The Performing
Troy   Amphitheater   Arts
Mount
Clemens
Great Lakes   Farmer's
75   Sports City   Market

Van Dyke   Airborne
Sports   Skate Park
Center   LAKE
Warren   3   ST. CLAIR

39   Madison
Heights   Eastpointe

Macomb
County

N

Macomb County

Just for Fun

Lionel Trains Visitor Center
50625 Richard W. Blvd.
Chesterfield Township, MI 48051
(586) 949-4100

A model train display at the Lionel Trains Visitors Center. Photo courtesy of Lionel Trains

I'm not sure if it's odd for a little girl to love model trains, but I certainly did. In fact, my father actually built my first set. As an adult I found it very interesting that the most famous of all model trains are made right in my home state!

From the time Joshua Lionel Cowen placed the first electrically powered car on a circle of track, individuals and entire families have joined together to experience the fun of model railroading. Lionel Trains have been collected by adults and children alike since the 1900s. The company has changed ownership several times; and in 1995, Wellspring Associates LLC and musician Neil Young acquired Lionel Trains from Richard Kughn. The Lionel Trains Visitor Center offers a free tour, which includes a ten-minute video on the company's production process and history. Visitors will see a fourteen-by-forty-foot set of tracks with ten running model trains, and will be encouraged to push various buttons controlling accessories. Smaller versions of the trains and tracks are available for tinier kids. The tour lasts from forty-five minutes to an hour. Of course, the gift shop is open during the tour, and I can't imagine leaving without picking up something. Unfortunately, the factory isn't part of the tour.

> **Lionel Trains Visitor Center**
>
> Cost: Tour is free, but reservations are required
>
> Hours: Call for tour times
>
> Directions: Exit I-94 at New Baltimore (#243), left on 23 Mile Road, left on Richard W. Blvd.

Chapter Four

Downtown Mount Clemens

Located on the winding banks of the Clinton River, Mount Clemens offers its residents small-town delights with the conveniences of contemporary urban life.

The central business and retail sections radiate from Macomb Street, featuring gazebos, water fountains, gardens, statuary, and shrubbery. Little coffee shops, delicatessens, restaurants, and pubs are abundant in the downtown district. It's easy to spend a day here window shopping, enjoying the lakeside parks, and trying some of the downtown restaurants.

Morley Candy Factory Tour

23700 Hall Road
Clinton Township, MI 48038
(800) 682-2760
www.morleycandy.com

Morley Candy Factory Tour

Hours: Tours, 10am & 1pm daily; self-guided tours, 7am–3:30pm, Mon–Fri.

Cost: Free.

Directions: Exit I-696 at Van Dyke Avenue (#23), head north on Van Dyke about 7 miles, continue on M-53 about 5 miles, take the 23 Mile Road exit, right on 23 Mile, left on Hayes, right on Hallmark Drive.

Give yourself and your kids a special sweet treat and schedule a tour of this famous candy-making mecca. Morley has made its name synonymous with delectable chocolate since 1919 and the tour offers a peek into its preparation and packaging. The guided tour lasts about an hour and twenty minutes and, of course, includes a chance to shop in the candy store and sample the wares.

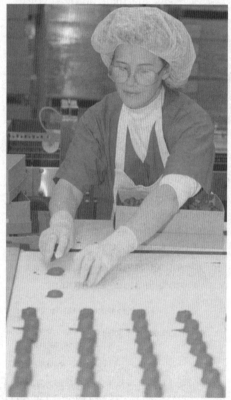

Sorting chocolates at Morley Candy.
Photo courtesy of C & G Newspapers

A Parent's Guide to

Southeastern Michigan

Macomb County

Mount Clemens Farmer's Market

Mount Clemens, MI 48043
(586) 493-7600

You'll find delicious apples and lots more at the Mount Clemens Farmer's Market.
Photo courtesy of C & G Newspapers

**Mount Clemens
Farmer's Market**

Hours: May–November
7am–2pm.

Directions: Exit I-94 at on North River Road. Market is at the Park and Ride Lot on North River Road, between I-94 and Gratiot.

For more than twenty years, the Mount Clemens Farmer's Market has provided a harvest of fresh food for area residents. Each month the market hosts seasonal themes, including flowers and fruits.

Chapter Four

The Art Center Gallery

125 Macomb Place
Mount Clemens, MI 48403
(586) 469-8666

The Art Center Gallery enhances the cultural atmosphere of this up-and-coming area. Shows change monthly, but many feature Michigan artists. Classes for kids and adults are offered frequently.

The Art Center Gallery

Hours: 11am–5pm, Tues–Fri; 9am–2pm, Sat; closed Sun–Mon.

Directions: Exit I-94 at Gratiot Avenue (#231), head north about 5 miles, left on Terry Street, right on Main Street, left on Macomb Place.

Hanna's Book Shop

61 Macomb Place
Mount Clemens, MI 48043
(586) 307-8810
www.hannasbookshop.com

This is a family-run bookstore with a nice children's selection and one of the best selections of periodicals for miles around. It's almost as big as the chain bookstores, but the atmosphere is definitely homier.

Hanna's Book Shop

Hours: 9am–6pm, Mon–Sat; closed Sunday; extended summer hours.

Directions: Exit I-94 at Gratiot Avenue (#231), head north about 5 miles, left on Terry Street, right on Main Street, left on Macomb Place.

Macomb Center for the Performing Arts

44575 Garfield Road
Clinton Township, MI 48038
www.macombcenter.com
(586) 286-2222

Each season the Macomb Center presents a lineup of 90 to100 professional events, including Broadway musicals, jazz, classical, and dance programs. The theater itself also happens to be gorgeous. There is

Macomb Center for the Performing Arts

Directions: Exit I-696 at Van Dyke Avenue, head north about 10 miles, take the M-59 exit east, turn right on Hall Road, right on Garfield Road.

4,000 square feet of "acoustic sculpture" (tiles created to enhance sound) on the theater's rear and side balcony walls reproduced from four designs by local artist Glen Michaels. Seats offer lots of leg space, clear views, and no one in the audience is farther than ninety feet from the stage. There is a noteworthy annual children's series and a discount family ticket package.

Macomb County

Joe Dumars' Fieldhouse

45300 Mound Road
Shelby Township, MI 48316
(586) 731-3080
www.joedumarsfieldhouse.com

Miniature golf is just one of the many activities at Joe Dumars' Fieldhouse. Photo courtesy of Joe Dumars' Fieldhouse

A sports megaplex that has become the area's fastest-growing destination event facility, Joe Dumars' Fieldhouse has something for the sports and game-minded alike. Not a surprise, considering its namesake is a former Detroit Pistons basketball player. Boasting a fitness center and first class athletic facilities for basketball, volleyball, in-line skating, and floor hockey, the Fieldhouse is a premier gym in a class of its own. In fact, it is home to the Detroit Roller Hockey Association, one of the largest roller hockey leagues in the United States. Kid-focused and kid-friendly, the Fieldhouse also offers a huge variety of sports camp programs year-round.

Chapter Four

Inside the Fieldhouse is the Bayou Fun Center, where the name says it all. (It really is decked out like the bayou and offers tons of fun.) Play eighteen holes of indoor miniature golf, climb a twenty-five–foot rock-climbing wall, zap friends and foes in the laser tag arena, shoot down the thirty-three foot inflatable Titanic Slide, and spend some coins in the arcade. Don't miss the High Ropes Course, where you can challenge yourself on an obstacle course that happens to be twenty to thirty feet in the air. Don't worry—you are in a harness, so injury is not an option.

> **Joe Dumars' Fieldhouse**
>
> Hours: Daily, 8am–2am; Bayou Fun Center, Sun–Thurs, 9am–10pm, and Fri–Sat, 9am–midnight
>
> Cost: Bayou Golf: $5.75; Caj'n Cliffs Climb: $3.75; Gator Tag: $4.50; Titanic Slide: $4.50
>
> Directions: Exit I-696 at Mound Road (#22), continue north about 10 miles.

Plaster Playhouse

43063 Hayes
Sterling Heights, MI 48313
(586) 566-0666

Express yourself in plaster and paint to create original art—from candlesticks to figures to mugs. Choose from a variety of sizes and shapes. Parties and field trips are available, too.

> **Plaster Playhouse**
>
> Directions: Exit I-696 at Groesbeck Highway (#26), left on Groesbeck, left on Utica Road, right on Hayes Road.

Macomb County

Airborne Skate Park

28070 Hayes Road
Roseville, MI 48066
(586) 776-7500
www.airbornesk8.com

A skater rides the bowl at Airborne. Photo courtesy of C & G Newspapers

There are definitely two camps of kids when it comes to recreation on wheels: Skateboarders and in-line skaters. Whatever your preference, you can roll here. It also holds special BMX cycling nights. The indoor skate park has an enviable layout, with a deep bowl and seemingly endless maze of ramps, rails, and quarter-pipes. Real skateboarding legends like Tony Hawk have been known to show up here.

Airborne Skate Park

Hours: Tues–Sat, noon–10pm; Sun, 11:30am–6pm; closed Mon.

Cost: Members skate: $6, members BMX bike: $10, nonmembers skate: $12, nonmembers BMX bike: $16.

Directions: Exit I-696 at Groesbeck Highway (#26), left on Groesbeck, left on Martin, right on Hayes.

Chapter Four

Freedom Hill Amphitheater

15000 Metropolitan Parkway
Sterling Heights, MI 48312
(586) 268-5100
www.palacenet.com

Nationally acclaimed acts perform at Freedom Hill all summer. Photo courtesy of C & G Newspapers

The intimate Freedom Hill Amphitheater provides stellar views from the lawn and pavilion. In the past, children's shows like "Franklin the Turtle and the Magic Fiddle" and "Little Bear and the Enchanted Wood" have graced the stage.

Freedom Hill Amphitheater

Directions: Exit I-696 at Van Dyke Avenue (#23), north on Van Dyke about 5 miles, right on Metropolitan Parkway.

Macomb County

Great Lakes Sports City

34400 Utica Road
Fraser, MI 48026
(586) 294-2400

Five full-size hockey rinks are the main attraction of this facility that also features a full-service pro shop, child-care, an arcade, concessions, and a bank. Leagues for all ages, drop-in hockey, and open skating are offered.

> **Great Lakes Sports City**
>
> Hours: Call for open skate times.
>
> Directions: Exit I-696 at Groesbeck Highway (#26), north on Groesbeck, left on Utica Road.

Metro Hoops

43655 Utica Road
Sterling Heights, MI 48314
(586) 731-4667

When it's too cold to play "Around the World" outside, head for Metro Hoops. Three basketball courts, volleyball, and youth and adult leagues are just a taste of what this Sterling Heights jock-haven has to offer. They host a variety of three-on-three tournaments, kids parties, activities, and clinics. If your kids are keen on learning the rules of hoops and you're a little, shall we say, athletically challenged, Metro Hoops offers programs geared to kids five to fourteen. Organized pickup teams can rent courts, too.

> **Metro Hoops**
>
> Hours: 10am–11pm daily.
>
> Directions: Exit I-696 at Van Dyke Avenue (#23), north on Van Dyke about 8 miles, left on Utica Road.

Van Dyke Sports Center

32501 Van Dyke Avenue
Warren, MI 48093
(586) 979-2626

When you can't bear to hear another, "Hey Mom! I'm bored!"—try heading to Van Dyke Sports Center. With the likes of a super arcade, twenty-seven pool tables, two mini golf courses, go-carts, a golf range, and a golf dome, it's highly unlikely you or the family will be bored here. The Sports Center offers a huge array of games for the kids, which makes it a good place to take them when the weather is inclement. The dome offers golf lessons as well.

> **Van Dyke Sports Center**
>
> Hours: 8am–2pm
>
> Directions: Exit I-696 at Van Dyke Avenue, head north.

Kart 2 Kart

42705 Van Dyke
Sterling Heights, MI 48314
(586) 997-8800
www.kart2kart.com

Take a spin in a go-cart at Kart 2 Kart. Photo courtesy of C & G Newspapers

An interesting high-tech go-cart track for kids and adults who are really kids at heart. Participants compete in 5.5 HP engines on a curved track against a timing system. Every safety precaution appears to be taken here. Group races can be arranged, too.

Kart 2 Kart

Hours: 11am–9pm, Mon–Wed; 11am–11pm Thurs–Fri; noon–9pm, Sun.

Cost: Varies, call for info.

Directions: Exit I-696 at Van Dyke Avenue, head north about 8 miles.

Special rules: Drivers must wear closed-toe shoes, be a minimum of 18 years old (or have a signed parental consent form) and be at least 5' tall.

Macomb County

Parking It

Stony Creek Metropark

4300 Main Park Road
Shelby Township, MI 48316
(800) 477-7756

Sarah gets her hands dirty while at a Stony Creek July 4 celebration.
Photo by Howard Lovy

With 4,461 acres, this is the largest metropark in the area. Boating and launch ramps; boat rental; swimming at two beaches; picnicking; a hike/bike trail; and an eighteen-hole, seventy-two-par public golf course should keep you and the kids occupied.

If you have any doubt, you might want to consider the twelve hours we enjoyed at Stony Creek during a recent July Fourth celebration. We packed up the girls with a picnic basket and spent the day hiking, playing frisbee, biking, swimming, and cruising around the lake in a paddleboat. At sunset, we spread out a blanket near the lake and were treated to a Motown-esque concert and spectacular fireworks. No one ever got bored or complained that they wanted to go home, and the only argument was over who was going to steer the paddleboat (I recommend you settle this BEFORE you're in the middle of the lake).

The hike and bike trail is a paved 6.2-mile loop circling Stony Creek Lake. Winter sports include ice fishing, sledding, tobogganing, traditional cross-country skiing, and ski rental service. Nature trails, open year-round, feature winter bird feeding stations and animal tracks. You really couldn't ask for more in a park.

Stony Creek Metropark

Hours: Winter, 8am–8pm; summer, 6am–10pm.

Cost: $2 Mon–Fri; $3 weekends; $15 annual pass.

Directions: Exit I-75 at Rochester Road (#67), right on Rochester about 7 miles, right on Avon Road, right on 25 Mile Road, left on Shelby Road, right on Main Park Drive.

Chapter Four

Four Bears Water Park

3000 Auburn Road
Utica, MI 48317
(586) 739-5860
www.fourbearswaterpark.com

Four Bears Water Park

Hours: 11am–7pm daily.

Cost: $12.95 all day admission; $5.95 under 48 inches; $5 nonparticipating chaperone; kids under 2 are free.

Directions: Exit I-696 at Dequindre Road (#20), north on Dequindre about 11 miles, right on Auburn Road.

With more than fifty acres, Four Bears could very well be the premier water park in these parts. Size notwithstanding, the squeals from refreshed, ecstatic children are proof of its fun factor. Splash down a triple water slide, get aggression out on bumper boats, and scream down the "speed slide." For the more docile, there's a petting zoo and a miniature golf course. A beach area surrounds the manmade lake where jet skis and paddleboats can be rented. If you seek a shady place for lunch, the picnic shelter is loaded with tables. An arcade, kiddie rides, and a go-cart track add to the list of reasons why Four Bears is a leading contender for those hazy days of summer. Check the website for special discounts and theme days.

Dodge Park

40400 Utica Road
Sterling Heights, MI 48313
(586) 446-2700

Dodge Park

Hours: Dawn-dusk.

Cost: Free.

Directions: Exit I-696 at Van Dyke Avenue, north on Van Dyke about 7 miles, right on 18 Mile Road, right on Utica Road.

Locals swear by this park. It's large without being unmanageable, yet somehow it still maintains the feel of a neighborhood park. Dodge Park stretches out lazily at the corner of Utica and Dodge Park roads. Perfect trails are plentiful for biking, blading, or walking and appreciating nature. The amphitheater hosts a variety of bands for summer concerts, where families and friends spread the beach blanket and park the lawn chairs. If the kids would rather run and climb, a huge playscape awaits them. For those who can bear the summer heat long enough for a volleyball workout, sand courts are available as well.

Macomb County

Metro Beach Metropark
31300 Metropolitan Parkway
Mount Clemens, MI 48046
(586) 463-4581

Metro Beach features an interactive waterpark for kids.
Photo courtesy of Huron-Clinton Metroparks

Metro Beach Metropark

Hours: 6am–10pm daily.

Cost: Requires vehicle entry pass: $15 yearly, $3 for the weekend, $2 for the day.

Directions: Exit I-696 at Groesbeck Highway (#26), north on Groesbeck, left on Utica Road, right on Metropolitan Parkway.

Metro Beach boasts activities that complement every extreme in Michigan's four seasons. The 770-acre park manages to accommodate both water lovers and fans of winter alike. Stroll along the 1,600-foot boardwalk for a magnificent view of Lake St. Clair just about any time of the year. Bring some binoculars and wow your kids with up-close views of freighters cutting through the lake en route to the Detroit River. In the summer, seven miles of beach overlook Lake St. Clair. Call ahead if you're planning on swimming, though. Unfortunately, high levels of lake bacteria sometimes close the beach. If chlorinated water is more appealing, an Olympic-sized swimming pool comes complete with a waterslide for a wet and wild day. A Tot Lot provides little tikes with an area to burn off excess energy. With boat launching facilities, Metro Beach's Marina is a definite hot spot in the summer for those who choose to watch the boats.

During the winter months, ice-skating and hockey are offered on lit rinks with a warm-up shelter where you can regain the feeling in your toes. Ice fishing and cross-country skiing throw in a nicely rounded winter month activity package. The Nature Center Building is open all year, providing nature trails into marshes and surrounding woods.

Chapter Four

Riverbends Park
At Auburn and Ryan roads
Utica, MI 48317
(586) 731-0300

Riverbends Park is lovely even in the winter. Photo courtesy of C & G Newspapers

This park is a living tribute to Michigan's history and that of the canal-building era of the mid-1800s. Officials who were eager to put the state on the map began an ambitious project to link Lake St. Clair with Lake Michigan. Digging on a shipping canal between the Clinton River and western Michigan's Kalamazoo began in 1838, but an economic depression soon forced an end to the vision. Today, remnants of the twelve miles of canal that were dug still exist, especially in the area of the park off Ryan Road. You can explore the canal and its tow path, walk more than ten miles of hiking and cross-country ski trails, or have a picnic.

Riverbends Park

Hours: 8am–8pm.

Hours: 8am–8pm, 7 days.

Cost: No admission fee.

Directions: Exit I-696 at Van Dyke Avenue, head north, left on 22 Mile Road. Park entrance between Ryan and Shelby roads.

Macomb County

Westview Orchards and Cider Mill

65075 Van Dyke
Romeo, MI 48095
(586) 752-3123
www.westvieworchards.com

Picking out the perfect pumpkin at Westview Orchard. Photo by Howard Lovy

Westview Orchards and Cider Mill

Hours: Vary by season, call or see website for details.

Directions: Exit I-696 at Van Dyke Avenue, head north for about seven miles' ; Van Dyke becomes M-53, continue north another 15 miles, left on 32 Mile Road, right on Prospect Street, left on Van Dyke Road.

This is truly closer to a carnival than a cider mill, but that's not exactly a bad thing. This won't be a quiet, leisurely day sipping hot cider and eating doughnuts with the kids. Instead, you'll be sipping hot cider, eating doughnuts, climbing a mountain of straw bales, feeding farm animals at the petting zoo, taking hay rides, and (if you dare) navigating your way through a maze carved into a cornfield. You get the picture?

That's not all there is to do here, either. There is a fantastic fruit and vegetable market, pony rides, a self-pick orchard, and the "Kidz Korner" play area. You can easily spend a day here when you factor in the special events held on fall weekends. We had fun in the seemingly never-ending pumpkin patch looking for the perfect carvers.

Chapter Four

For Inquisitive Minds

Michigan Transit Museum

200 Grand Ave.
Mount Clemens, MI 48043
(586) 463-1863

It's not exactly a stretch to say that this little building changed the course of history. To understand why, you must know that a young Thomas Edison spent a great deal of time at this former train depot when he was a railway newsboy on the Detroit to Port Huron line. He got to know the station agent, and in 1862, he saved the agent's son from being killed by a rolling boxcar. In gratitude, the agent taught Edison telegraphy, a skill that figured into his earliest inventions. The depot was still in use until 1980, when it was sold and turned into a museum. Since then, it has been restored—inside you'll find exhibits on railroad history, and a gift shop with some great conversation pieces.

> **Michigan Transit Museum**
>
> Hours: 1pm–4pm, Sat–Sun
>
> Directions: Exit I-696 at Groesbeck Highway (#26), head north about 8 miles, right on Cass Avenue, left on Grand Avenue.

Macomb County

Selfridge Military Air Museum and Air Park

27333 C Street, Building 1011
Mount Clemens, MI 48045
(586) 307-5035
www.selfridgeairmuseum.org

The HH-52A Seaguard, part of the historic aircraft display at Selfridge Military Air Museum.
Photo courtesy of Selfridge

> **Selfridge Military Air Museum and Air Park**
>
> Hours: noon–4pm, Saturday–Sunday.
>
> Cost: Free, donation suggested.
>
> Directions: Exit I-94 at Harper Road (#234B), right on Harper, right on Klix Street, right on Shook Road, left on Jefferson Avenue, left on Lakeview Boulevard, left on Cape Lane.

One of the nation's oldest, most historic military bases offers a museum with military memorabilia and twenty-three different aircraft displays. Children can learn the history of the base, and see the various models and diagrams of historical military aircraft. Because this is a working military facility, it is best to call ahead for current specific hours, access requirements, and registration when necessary.

Frontier Town

67380 Van Dyke Road
Romeo, MI 48065
(586) 752-6260

> **Frontier Town**
>
> Hours: 11am–6pm daily.
>
> Directions: Exit I-696 at Van Dyke Avenue (#23), head north about 21 miles, left on 31 Mile Road, right on Van Dyke Road, south on Main Street.

Catch a glimpse of the Western past at this ten-acre attraction on the east side of town. The only thing missing here are cowboy shoot-outs (there are no reenactments here). Visit a toy store or a Christmas-all-the-time shop. If you need a sugar fix, there's an old-fashioned ice cream parlor and candy store. During the Christmas season, Santa comes to visit, via helicopter. I'm not kidding. Of course, no Western complex would be complete without a petting farm for the little ones to visit. You might want to keep this place in mind for a Sunday drive destination—kids really do seem to love it.

Chapter Four

Wolcott Mill Metropark

**63841 Wolcott Road
Ray, MI 48096
(586) 749-5997**

This metropark is so scenic in the fall, that you'll often find armies of tripods lined up, hoping to catch that perfect shot. Visit an 1847 grist mill, play eighteen holes of golf, or watch the daily milking of the dairy herd. There are two hiking trails and a ten-mile equestrian trail for horse lovers.

Wolcott Mill Metropark

Hours: 6am–10pm daily; Farm Learning Center is open 9am–5pm daily.

Cost: Requires vehicle entry pass: $15 yearly, $3 for the weekend, $2 for the day.

Directions: Exit I-696 at Van Dyke Avenue (#23). Head north about 20 miles, bear left on Van Dyke Road, right on 29 Mile Road, left on Wolcott Road.

The 1847 grist mill at Wolcott. Photo courtesy of Huron-Clinton Metroparks

Southeastern Michigan

Chapter Five

Washtenaw County

In Washtenaw County, it's convenient and feasible to take a kayak out in the morning, stop at an art gallery later, and then join about 100,000 other sports fanatics for a University of Michigan football game. You can't do this anywhere else in the state, and that's just a miniscule sampling of what this diverse, urban, *and* rural area has to offer.

The 2000 U.S. Census reported about 323,000 residents living in this 710-square-mile county. That makes it nearly as large as Oakland County, with about one-third the people. You wouldn't know it by visiting the very walkable downtown Ann Arbor on any given weekend—the streets and sidewalk cafes are jam-packed. But the parks in town and cities just a short distance away provide a nice, calm setting for family activities. It's situated about thirty miles west of Detroit and boasts four cities: Ann Arbor, Ypsilanti, Saline, and Milan; and four villages: Chelsea, Manchester, Dexter, and Barton Hills.

Established in 1827, there are several legends about how Washtenaw County was named. Some believe it was the name of a Native American who lived near the mouth of the Huron River. Others think it was the Potawatami word for "river" or "large stream." Emerson Greenman, a former curator of the University of Michigan Museum of Anthropology, believes the name derived from the Algonquin term for "far country," with Detroit being the point of reference.

Chapter Five

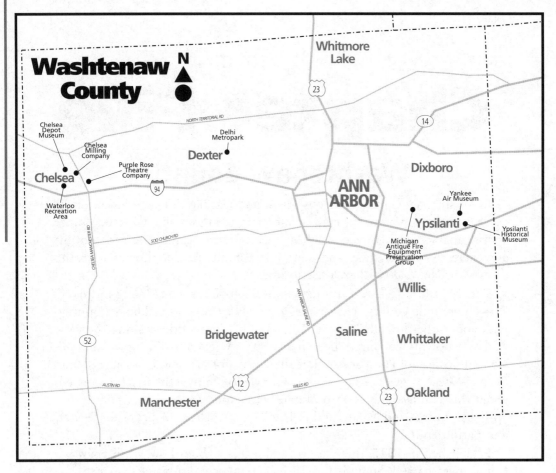

Whichever legend holds true, Washtenaw County is a mere jaunt from the Detroit area. It's only about a forty-five-minute drive and is the destination point for many families we know. In fact, my husband commutes from the Detroit area to Ann Arbor every day, but we enjoy the area so much we frequently take day trips with the kids. Whether it's Big Ten sports, one of the largest street art fairs in the United States, an internationally recognized medical center, or the lush parks that border the Huron River, Washtenaw County has something for everyone.

A Parent's Guide to

Southeastern Michigan

Washtenaw County

Just for Fun

Downtown Ann Arbor

Arts and entertainment for all ages abound in this city, so much so that it's safe to say that Ann Arbor is one of the most family-friendly downtown areas in all of Michigan. You could spend a lifetime checking out the works of artists who call Ann Arbor home, as well as the touring acts, and still not get to everything.

Downtown Ann Arbor

Directions: From the Metro Detroit area, take I-696 west to I-275 south, merge onto M-14 west (#45), then take U.S. 23 south to the downtown Ann Arbor exit (#3).

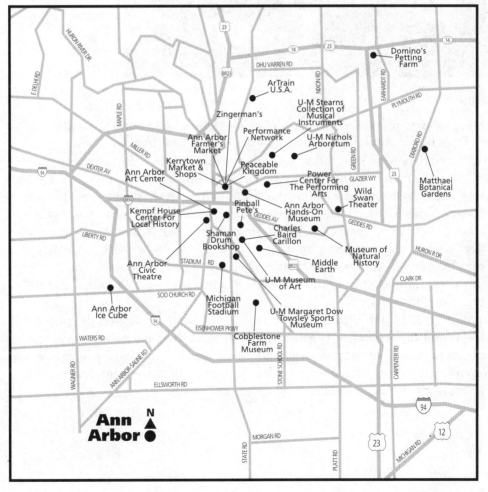

Chapter Five

Downtown Ann Arbor restaurants offer lots of sidewalk cafes.
Photo courtesy of Ann Arbor Area Convention and Visitors Bureau

In 1823, a crew of pioneers traveled through Detroit and continued along the banks of the Huron River in search of a location for a new frontier community. Among the settlers were John Allen and Elisha Rumsey. About forty miles west of Detroit, near the Huron River, the pioneers established their settlement. On Feb. 12, 1824, they registered their claims in Detroit—Allen for 480 acres and Rumsey for 160—each paying $1.25 per acre. Anyone currently shopping for real estate in the area will assure you these prices have since risen a tad; Ann Arbor rivals cities like New York and San Francisco in occupancy and cost. In May 1824, the settlers decided to name the town after their wives, Ann and Mary Ann. The "arbor" probably came into being from the tremendous amount of lush flora that can still be found along the river.

On May 25, 1824, the Wayne County Register of Deeds registered the plan for the village, and the settlement began to grow. In 1837 the University of Michigan was moved to Ann Arbor from Detroit and established on a forty-acre site. The school now occupies about a gazillion times that much and is an integral part of the community's culture, economic well-being, and flavor.

Washtenaw County

While there are loads of other incredibly worthwhile neighborhoods in the city, the most walkable two that you won't want to miss in downtown Ann Arbor are the Main Street area and the South University district. It's a pleasant stroll from one tree-lined district to another through the center of campus along the "Diag," a wide sidewalk that cuts right through many of the beautiful old University of Michigan buildings. From Main Street, walk east on Liberty or Washington to State Street, then south to the Diag. There are plenty of places to stop and rest if younger ones get tired; one of our favorite places is **Stucchi's Ice Cream, 302 S. State Street.**

Pinball Pete's

1214 S. University Avenue
Ann Arbor, MI 48104
(734) 213-2502

If you have a gamer in the family, no trip to Ann Arbor would be complete without a stop at Pinball Pete's. But be warned: Time flies in this dark arcade, and hours can easily slip by as you and the kids play the latest video games, pool, or old-school-style pinball. There is an older crowd—students and other locals—who tend to hang out here at night, so you might want to tag along to supervise younger kids. Our friend John, who is comfortably in his early thirties, loves Pete's and feels at home there playing his favorite "classic" video game, Tempest.

Pinball Pete's

Hours: 10am–2am every day.

Directions: From M-14, take Main Street south to Packard Street, turn left, left on Madison, left on State, right on University.

Chapter Five

Shaman Drum Bookshop

311 S. State Street
Ann Arbor, MI 48104
(800) 490-7023
www.shamandrum.com

Shaman Drum Bookshop

Hours: 10am–10pm, Mon–Sat;
noon–6pm, Sun

Directions: From M-14, take Main
Street south to William Street, turn
left, left on State.

Though they specialize in scholarly books in the humanities and literature, the Shaman Drum has a pleasant children's area. Truth is, this indie bookshop is more likely to please Mom and Dad or older kids, but the children's section is vast enough to keep young ones busy while the grownups browse. We keep a lookout for special events here, as many interesting authors on book tours stop in for readings.

Borders

612 E. Liberty Street
Ann Arbor, MI 48104
(734) 668-7100

Borders

Hours: 9am–11pm, Mon–Sat;
9am–9 p.m. Sun.

Directions: From M-14, take Main
Street south to Depot Street, turn
left, right on State, right on Liberty.

There are now hundreds of Borders stores across the U.S. and overseas, but this one is noteworthy because it's the original—well, actually it's about a block away from the original. When Tom and Louis Borders opened their first store here in 1971, they were essentially creating one of the first book superstores. What you'll find today is a huge, two-story building full of enough books, periodicals, and music to keep you and your family busy for hours on a rainy or snowy day. The children's area is enormous, the staff is knowledgeable and helpful, and the cafe offerings are impressive.

Kerrytown Market and Shops

415 N. Fifth Avenue
Ann Arbor, MI 48104
(734) 662-5008
kerrytown.com

Kerrytown Market and Shops

Hours: Open 7 days, call individual stores for hours.

Directions: From M-14, take Main
Street south to Kingsley Street, turn
left, right on Fifth Avenue.

It's entirely possible to spend half a day in the small section of Ann Arbor that houses Kerrytown. This eclectic collection of more than twenty shops and restaurants is housed in a trio of century-old factory and warehouse buildings. I find this to be a pleasant departure from mall shopping. Unique shops and cafes are a treat to discover as you walk around the old, squeaky floors of these great old structures.

Washtenaw County

The Kitchen Port, (800) 832-7678, is just the place to take a young, budding chef to look for cool gadgets and books; **Mudpuddles**, (734) 662-0022, has a variety of one-of-a-kind toys that you'll never find at chains; and Vintage to Vogue has home accessories and furniture to help make any room in the house stylish.

Ann Arbor Farmer's Market

315 Detroit Street
Ann Arbor, MI 48104
(734) 994-3276

> **Ann Arbor Farmer's Market**
>
> Hours: May–December, Wed & Sat, 7am–3pm; January–April, Saturday only, 8am–3 pm.
>
> Directions: Located adjacent to Kerrytown Market and Shops.

While I'm a self-confessed farmer's market junkie and probably a little biased when it comes to describing them (I love them all), this one is exceptional. Early risers can choose from the best of the area's produce, baked goods, plants, and cut flowers. Offerings change with the seasons, of course, but the locally produced fare is always fresh, varied, and plentiful. Sundays here are a treat, too. The Ann Arbor Sunday Artisans Market offers up a variety of crafts, including pottery, furniture, clothing, and photography. The Artisans Market is held 11:00 a.m. to 4:00 p.m., Sundays only, May through December.

Pick up a bouquet along with fresh veggies at the Kerrytown Farmer's Market.
Photo courtesy of Ann Arbor Area Convention and Visitors Bureau

Chapter Five

Zingerman's

422 Detroit Street
Ann Arbor, MI 48104
(734) 663-DELI
www.zingermans.com

Zingerman's

Hours: 7am–10pm daily

Directions: From M-14, take Main Street south to Kingsley Street, turn left, right on Fifth Avenue, left on Detroit Street.

This has long been a family favorite with us. My parents always made it a stop when we visited the Ann Arbor street art fairs, and now my husband and I enjoy taking the girls here as frequently as possible for a New York–style deli feast. Just a pickle's toss from the Kerrytown Market and Shops, Zingerman's is the perfect stop for dinner after a day shopping on Main Street or playing and discovering at the Hands-On Museum.

The long lines can be daunting at times, but the food is superb and well worth the wait. What's always been amazing to us is that no matter how intensely busy the deli gets, the staff is never flustered, always cheery, and incredibly patient with little ones who may be overwhelmed with all the choices. During warm weather, there is a cool children's play area situated off the side of the patio. Beyond its whopper sandwiches and scrumptious brownies, Zingerman's has a grocery section with gourmet treats second to none in the state.

Indulge in the variety of yummy New York deli-style treats at Zingerman's.
Photo courtesy of Ann Arbor Area Convention and Visitors Bureau

Washtenaw County

Peaceable Kingdom

210 S. Main Street
Ann Arbor, MI 48104
(734) 668-7886

Peaceable Kingdom

Hours: 10am–6pm, Mon–Thurs;
10am–9pm, Fri; 10 am –6 pm Sat;
closed Sun.

Directions: From M-14, take Main
Street south into downtown Ann
Arbor. The store is between
Washington and Liberty.

Peaceable Kingdom is just plain fun for adults and kids. The long, narrow boutique has some higher-end jewelry, crafts, and gifts on its shelves, but down the middle of the store is a row of wooded bins, loaded with an amazing array of odd, inexpensive stuff. My husband and I enjoy ourselves as much as the girls do, digging through the mini fold-up fans, bug boxes, flip books, chattering plastic teeth, and dozens of miniature plastic animals. You can walk out the door having spent no more than five dollars and have a bag full of goodies for the kids.

Middle Earth

1209 S. University Avenue
Ann Arbor, MI 48104
(734) 769-1488

Middle Earth

Hours: 10am–7pm, Mon–Thurs;
10am–8pm, Fri; 10am–7pm, Sat.;
noon–6pm, Sun.

Directions: From M-14, take Main
Street south to Packard Street, turn
left, left on Madison, left on State,
right on University.

This is more than a novelty shop—it's a gift shop with a tremendous sense of humor. Named for the world created by J.R.R. Tolkien in his trilogy (though it doesn't seem to carry much related stuff, last time we checked), Middle Earth allows the eclectic shopper to leave with a bright pink, life-sized candle in the form of a hand, some Mexican Day of the Dead–styled lanterns, and a "Fat Albert" T-shirt. There are some beautiful imported and local crafts and jewelry here, as well. And that's just the beginning. You may want to steer younger kids away from the rather risqué greeting card selection, but everyone in the family is bound to get a chuckle or two from the nifty merchandise stocked here.

Chapter Five

Ann Arbor Ice Cube

2121 Oak Valley Drive
Ann Arbor, MI 48103
(734) 213-1600

You can partake in just about everything there is to do on ice here, except fish. Three ice rinks allow for open skating, figure skating lessons, broomball, amateur hockey, and physical therapy. The center also features a pro shop, fitness center, cafe, and arcade. If you can't keep your kids off skates, you might want to consider throwing their next birthday party here. Reserve an entire ice rink and watch them become the envy of all their friends.

> **Ann Arbor Ice Cube**
>
> Hours: Vary by activities and events, call ahead.
>
> Cost: Daily public skating, adults $4, kids 12 and under $3; skate rental $3.
>
> Directions: Exit I-94 at Ann Arbor Saline Road (#175), turn left, right on Waters Road, right on Oak Valley Drive.

Wild Swan Theater

416 W. Huron Parkway
Ann Arbor, MI 48103
(734) 995-0530
www.comnet.org/wildswan

Wild Swan is a professional theater that performs for family audiences, and there are several of those in Southeastern Michigan. What makes this troupe so exceptional is the great effort made to accommodate children with disabilities. There is plenty of space in the audience for those using wheelchairs and other mobility devices, but that's not all. Audio descriptions and backstage visits prior to performances are encouraged for kids who are blind or visually impaired. Kids are able to touch costumes, masks, and puppets that will be used during performances, so they're better able to enjoy themselves. Also, American Sign Language interpreting is woven seamlessly into every performance. Classics such as *The Wizard of Oz* and *Peter Rabbit* are often on the schedule, but so are educational performances like *Along the Tracks: Michigan and the Underground Railroad*.

> **Wild Swan Theater**
>
> Hours: Vary by performance.
>
> Cost: Children $6; adults $8.
>
> Directions: From M-14, take Main Street to West Huron, turn right.

Washtenaw County

Afternoon Delight Cafe

251 E. Liberty Street
Ann Arbor, MI 48104
(734) 665-7513

If you're looking for a quick meal on the run and you have the kids in tow, this is a great choice. Afternoon Delight offers four daily homemade soups, fresh baked muffins and breads, healthy sandwiches, and an amazing salad bar. The bonanza bagel is toasted and slathered with peanut butter, then topped with bananas, sunflower seeds, and honey. Most entrees are less than $6. For lunch, the huge, stuffed baked potatoes are perfect for kids. This cafe has one of the most unique breakfast menus in the area, which it serves all day on weekends.

Ann Arbor Art Center

117 W. Liberty Street
Ann Arbor, MI 48104
(734) 994-8004
www.annarborartcenter.org

Who says you have to paint with a brush? Photo courtesy of the Ann Arbor Art Center

Chapter Five

Sunday workshops are the highlight here, with projects like mosaic plate-making, floor murals, and more. No artistic talent is needed, so most kids will be able to relax and be creative. Let the inner artist in your child run wild here; you never know what might happen. The center offers hands-on art education, art appreciation programs, and juried exhibitions. Group parties can be arranged and the Art Center has a popular summer camp. Studio classes in ceramics, drawing, painting, and jewelry are offered throughout the year, as well.

> **Ann Arbor Art Center**
>
> Hours: Workshops are held every Sunday at 1:00 p.m. (first Sundays of the month are free).
>
> Directions: From M-14, take Main Street south to Liberty, turn right.

Ann Arbor Civic Theatre

408 W. Washington Street
Ann Arbor, MI 48104
(734) 971-0605

We've found that kids seem to really enjoy the intimate setting of community theater, and it's a great introduction to performances if you're planning to attend a Broadway-scale production with them later. The Civic Theatre is more than a half-century old and produces plays for adults and kids. Check the website or call ahead for schedules.

> **Ann Arbor Civic Theatre**
>
> Hours: Performances generally scheduled for 2pm and 8pm.
>
> Cost: Varies by performance; average ticket price range is $5–$18.
>
> Directions: From M-14, take Main Street south to Washington, turn right.

Washtenaw County

Power Center for the Performing Arts

121 Fletcher Street
Ann Arbor, MI 48109
(734) 763-3333
www.theatre.music.umich.edu/uprod/facilities/power/power-home.html

This architecturally stunning 1,380-seat structure hosts music, dance, and theater performances all year. During its annual summer festival, acts from all over the world perform, some of which are great for the entire family. Also during the summer festival, Top of the Park has the allure of a picnic fantasy: films, live music, and gourmet food are offered in a relatively family-friendly environment on top of a surprisingly pretty parking structure adjacent to the Power Center. If it's a nice night, expect crowds.

> **Power Center for the Performing Arts**
>
> Directions: From M-14, take Main Street south to Huron Street, turn left, right on Fletcher.

The Top of the Park summer festival adjacent to the Power Center. Photo courtesy of Ann Arbor Area Convention and Visitors Bureau

Chapter Five

Performance Network

120 E. Huron Street
Ann Arbor, MI 48104
(734) 663-0681
comnet.org/PNetwork/

Performance Network
Directions: From M-14, take Main Street south to Ann Street, turn left, right on Fourth Avenue, right on Huron.

While the space is small (about 120 seats), this nonprofit, professional theater's contemporary plays are highly regarded by local critics. Most shows are more adult-oriented, but other family-friendly productions, like *Man of La Mancha*, show up from season to season. Children's theater productions are traveling only.

ArTrain U.S.A.

1100 N. Main Street
Ann Arbor, MI 48104
(734) 747-8300
www.artrainusa.org

ArTrain U.S.A.
Hours: Check the website or call ahead to see if ArTrain is in town and what the current exhibit is.
Cost: Free, donation suggested.
Directions: From M-14, take Main Street south, ArTrain will be on the left.

ArTrain is the nation's only truly mobile art museum. The train is headquartered in Ann Arbor but visits communities throughout the United States all year, so it's best to call for local visitation schedule or check the website. Inspired by Helen Milliken, a former Michigan first lady, ArTrain was founded in 1971 by the Michigan Council for the Arts as an outreach program to take art to Michigan communities that did not have access to metropolitan museums. The idea stuck. As you're driving into downtown Ann Arbor from the expressway, it's always a treat to see the brightly painted train pulled up at its home on Main Street.

Washtenaw County

Domino's Petting Farm

24 Frank Lloyd Wright Drive
Ann Arbor, MI 48106
(734) 998-0182
www.pettingfarm.com

Kids can interact with the animals at Domino's Petting Farm. Photo courtesy of Ann Arbor Area Convention and Visitors Bureau

Set in the beautifully scenic countryside (albeit surrounded by interstate highways) complete with duck pond and open pastures, Domino's Petting Farm provides great family fun, education, and entertainment. Built in 1925, the historic farmhouse and grounds are operated and maintained by a non-profit organization. Kids can pet the rare breed animals, watch an animal demonstration or enjoy a hayride. You can also visit the website and check the dates to plan your visit when the next babies are born. Group tours can be accommodated by reservation. Season passes are also available.

Domino's Petting Farm

Hours: All year, 9:30am–4pm, Mon–Fri; 10:30am–5pm, Sat–Sun.

Cost: Adults $4.50; seniors $4; and kids 2–12, $3.75 ($14.50 max per family of two parents and immediate children); children under 2 free.

Directions: Take US-23 to Exit 41 (Plymouth Road), go east 1/4 mile to Earhart Road, north on Earhart Road 1 mile.

107

Chapter Five

Chelsea

Charming downtown Chelsea is about sixteen miles west of downtown Ann Arbor. This is a quaint, walkable area that boasts some interesting boutiques, galleries, cafes, and antique shops. Minutes from downtown is the Waterloo Recreation Area, the largest state park in Michigan (see info in the "Parking It" section).

Chelsea Milling Company

201 W. North Street
Chelsea, MI 48118
(734) 475-1361
www.jiffymix.com

> **Chelsea Milling Company**
>
> Hours: The one- to 1 1/2 tours are held from 9am–1:30pm, Mon.-Fri.
>
> Cost: Free
>
> Directions: From I-94 west, take the Jackson Road/Old U.S. 12 exit (#162), right on M-52/Main Street, left on North Street.

What kid (or adult, for that matter) doesn't love a tour that ends with a treat? Here you can visit the site where the ever-popular Jiffy Mix is produced, check out the production aspects, and then munch on a delicious baked treat on your way out. And the company that makes America's first prepared baking mix still does everything here, from milling the wheat to making their own little blue boxes.

Boxes of Jiffy Mix whiz by at the Chelsea Milling Company. Photo courtesy of Ann Arbor Area Convention and Visitors Bureau

Washtenaw County

Chelsea Farmer's Market

Municipal parking lot in downtown Chelsea
Chelsea, MI 48118
(734) 433-0354

There are typically between fifteen and twenty-five food and craft vendors here on Saturdays, which turns out to be a huge amount for this cute little city. Along with the plethora of foods and crafts, the market provides some fun children's activities like face painting, crafts, and sidewalk chalk projects.

> **Chelsea Farmer's Market**
>
> Hours: May–October, 8am–noon, Sat.
>
> Directions: From I-94 west, take the Main Street/Chelsea exit, right on M-52/Main Street, right on Park, turn right into parking lot, farmer's market is on the left.

Purple Rose Theatre Company

137 Park Street
Chelsea, MI 48118
(734) 433-7673
www.purplerosetheatre.org

Actor Jeff Daniels created this nonprofit theater so Midwestern actors and playwrights could stay close to home. Years ago, when he began convert-

> **Purple Rose Theatre Company**
>
> Directions: From I-94 west, take the Main Street/Chelsea exit, right on M-52/Main Street, right on Park.

ing the old bus garage in downtown Chelsea, he received some negative reaction from critics (who preferred to see the latest shows from New York featuring his "movie star friends") and locals (who thought "art was someone who lived out by the highway"). His vision has succeeded thus far. Most performances are set in Middle America, or have themes of life in the region. The professional-caliber shows fill up fast, so make sure to book ahead of time. Student matinee performances at special prices are offered for appropriate shows throughout each season. Tours and theater workshops for kids are local favorites, too.

Chapter Five

University of Michigan (U-M)

Even if you're not an alumnus, you'd be hard pressed to find a Michiganian who said they didn't enjoy some aspect of this gorgeous campus (unless you're from rival Michigan State University, perhaps). To say the University of Michigan is an integral part of the city of Ann Arbor would be an understatement. It shapes the composition of the city's economy, population, and cultural awareness. About one of every three adults in the city is employed by the university, its worldwide reputation draws esteemed professors from all parts of the world, and the university hosts a wide range of cultural events promoting local and visiting artists, musicians, writers, and celebrities. University of Michigan sporting events draw thousands of enthusiastic spectators from all over.

See more U-M listings in the "For Inquisitive Minds" section in this chapter.

Michigan Football Stadium
Intersection of Main Street and Stadium Drive
University of Michigan
Ann Arbor, MI 48103
(734) 647-2583

The crowd gets revved up at a U-M football game. Photo by Doris Kraushaar

Washtenaw County

If you're a family of college football fans, a Saturday afternoon at Michigan Stadium is a must. The "Big House," as it's often called, seats just shy of 108,000 Wolverine fiends, many of whom will sport the oddest displays of the home team's colors—maize and blue —on any given game day. From argyle sweaters over the shoulders to body paint, you'll see it here.

From the outside, the stadium doesn't look too imposing, primarily since the field is sunken and about seventy rows of seats are below ground. Inside, however, there is no mistaking the enormity of it all, and the noise is deafening when the home team takes the field, particularly if a rival like Michigan State or Ohio State is in town. This is a different scene than, say, a Detroit Tiger's game, so if your kids are still young enough to be frightened by huge, enthusiastic crowds and extreme noise, you might want to find a sitter.

Tickets are attainable but should be purchased long before the season opener as games are always sold out. Always...I'm not kidding.

The stadium is located on the southwest portion of campus. Crisler Arena (home of Wolverine basketball) is right next door, and the stadium is within easy walking distance of the Michigan Union and other campus points of interest.

U-M Margaret Dow Towsley Sports Museum

Schembechler Hall
1200 S. State Street
Ann Arbor, MI 48109
(734) 763-4422

> **U-M Margaret Dow Towsley Sports Museum**
> Hours: 11am–4pm Mon–Fri.
>
> Directions: From M-14, take Main Street south to Depot Street, turn left, right on Carey Street, right on State.

This museum captures the tradition and spirit of more than 100 years of athletic competition at U-M. Exhibits share the story of Michigan athletes as part of the Rose Bowl, Big Ten Championship, and U.S. Olympic teams. You can view a short film, check out the exhibits, and have fun on the touch-screen computer features.

Chapter Five

U-M Stearns Collection of Musical Instruments

Saarenin Design School of Music
1100 Bates Drive
Ann Arbor, MI 48109
(734) 763-4389

More than 2,000 musical instruments have been acquired since Frederick Stearns (1831–1907), a Detroit businessman, donated the original collection of 940 pieces in 1899, making this one of the largest, most distinctive collections from around the world. If your kids are even a little musically inclined, this massive collection may be just the inspiration they need.

> **U-M Stearns Collection of Musical Instruments**
>
> Hours: 10am–5pm, Mon–Fri, or by arranged private tour.
>
> Cost: Free.
>
> Directions: From U.S. 23 take the Plymouth/Ann Arbor Road Exit, continue of Plymouth Road, left on Murfin Avenue, right on Duffield Street, left on Baits Drive.

Parking It

Delhi Metropark

3780 W. Delhi Road
Dexter, MI 48105
(734) 426-8211

> **Delhi Metropark**
>
> Hours: 8am–10pm, Memorial Day–Labor Day; 8am–9pm, rest of the year.
>
> Cost: Daily $4 car permit, annual $20.
>
> Directions: From M-14, take the Maple Road/Miller Road exit (#2), right on Miller, right on Wagner, left on Huron River Drive, left on Delhi.

This is a beautiful, wide-open park with lots of room to run around in. The fifty-acre park is about five miles northwest of downtown Ann Arbor. It runs along the Huron River and features two picnic shelters, fishing, a children's playscape, and canoe rentals. There is a terrific hiking path along the river, and we actually spent several hours there one day with the girls, just walking and watching the fish.

A canoe ride is a pleasant way to spend the afternoon— and test your coordination!
Photo courtesy of Huron-Clinton Metroparks

Washtenaw County

Matthaei Botanical Gardens

University of Michigan
1800 N. Dixboro Road
Ann Arbor, MI 48105
(734) 998-7060
www.lsa.umich.edu/mb

Matthaei Botanical Gardens
Hours: Conservatory: 10am–4:30pm, seven days; outside walkways open every day 8am–sunset.
Cost: Outside walkways free; conservatory entrance, adults $3; kids (K–12) $1.
Directions: From M-14, take the Ford Road/M-153 exit (#10), continue east on Ford Road, right on Plymouth Road, left on Dixboro.

This thirty-five-acre oasis is a favorite place for U-M students to take their parents when they come to visit. It's also a neat place for a first date or a great way to introduce your youngster to the wonders of nature. The gardens include marked hiking trails of various lengths, landscaped gardens, and an extensive multiclimate conservatory housing plants of botanical interest from all part of the globe— a wonderful getaway from nasty, cold winter weather.

The U-M Matthaei Botanical Gardens. Photo courtesy of Ann Arbor Area Convention and Visitors Bureau

Chapter Five

U-M Nichols Arboretum

1610 Washington Heights
Ann Arbor, MI 48104
(734) 998-9540

U-M Nichols Arboretum

Hours: Sunrise–Sunset.

Cost: Free.

Directions: From U.S. 23, take the Plymouth Road exit (#41), right on Plymouth Road, left on Huron Parkway, left on Geddes, right on Nichols, continue on Washington Heights.

Often described as a "123-acre living museum," the Arb is nestled in the hills adjacent to U-M's Central Campus and has a collection of about 600 different species of plants and trees. Truly a wonderful place to visit any time of the year, the Arb holds almost every species of plant found in Michigan. A leisurely stroll will take you through its flower gardens, forest areas, and luxurious meadows. Bike or walk along the winding Huron River. You might be able to wow the kids with the historic peony garden of almost 300 varieties (it's stunning), the Heathdale Collection of Appalachian plants, or the fifteen-acre Dow Prairie. Maps are available at the Arb's three entrances and various locations on the U-M campus.

Waterloo Recreation Area

16345 McClure Road
Chelsea, MI 48118
(734) 475-8307

Waterloo Recreation Area

Directions: From I-94, take the Old U.S. 12/Pierce Road exit (#157). Continue on Pierce Road, left on Cavanaugh Lake Road, right on Glazier Road, right on Lowery, left on McClure.

The impressive size of Waterloo earns it the largest park in Michigan's Lower Peninsula award: with more than 20,000 acres, it boasts eleven lakes, forty-seven miles of hiking trails, and three campgrounds. Pretty nice, considering that it's only about an hour's drive from most locations in suburban Detroit. Plentiful fishing, swimming on Big Portage Lake, and seemingly endless hiking, bicycle, and equestrian trails add to the allure of this park. More than 380 campsites encompassing the park's Sugarloaf, Portage Lake, and Green Lake campgrounds offer a varied camping experience ranging from rustic to modern to equestrian. Our experience with camping here wasn't exactly successful: The campgrounds fill quickly and become very crowded. We're more of the middle-of-nowhere type campers, but many people swear by this place. The Gerald E. Eddy Discovery Center, open year-round in the park, offers programs designed to educate visitors about the intricacies of Michigan's ecosystem and geological history. The center offers guided tours for groups, which must be arranged in advance.

Washtenaw County

Gallup Park

3000 Fuller Road
Ann Arbor, MI 48105
(734) 662-9319

Gallup Park

Directions: From U.S. 23 take the Geddes Road exit (#39), right on Geddes, continue on Fuller.

I guess the question here is: What can't you do at Gallup Park? You can rent paddleboats, canoes, bicycles, and fishing supplies. There are paved nature trails for hikers, bikers, and in-line skaters, and there are plenty of picnic shelters and restrooms to accommodate crowds of visitors at once. This is important, since this seems to be one of Ann Arbor's most popular parks. Even when there is a parking lot full of cars, we've been able to enjoy pleasant, quiet walks. It's ever so scenic, too. Arched footbridges connect a series of small islands, and a path connects Gallup to Parker Mill and the Forest Nature Area.

It's no secret that Gallup Park is a great spot for a picnic. Photo courtesy of Ann Arbor Area Convention and Visitors Bureau

115

Chapter Five

Rolling Hills County Park

7660 Stony Creek Road
Ypsilanti, MI 48197

It's probably impossible to get bored at this park, and if you do, you're not trying hard enough. Kids can burn off energy on 150 acres in a water park, on nature trails, or even a fishing pond. A nine-hole disc golf course presents an enticing challenge, so don't forget your frisbee. Winter fun is prominent here, too. There's a perfect sledding hill (tube and toboggan rentals are available), natural ice skating pond, and groomed cross-country ski trails. To warm those chilly toes, take advantage of the cozy fireplace in the lodge.

Rolling Hills County Park

Winter ski info: (734) 484-9676.

Water park info: (734) 484-9655.

Hours: 8am–dusk.

Cost: Vehicle entrance fees: $6 daily pass for nonresidents, $3 for Washtenaw County residents; $36 annual pass for nonresidents, $18 for residents. Waterpark entrance: $4 day rate weekdays, $5 weekends. Locker rental 25 cents; tube rental $1.

Directions: From I-94, take the Huron Street exit (#183), left on Hamilton Street, right on Stony Creek Road.

Dexter-Huron Metropark

6535 Huron River Drive
Dexter, MI 48130
(734) 426-8211

Pack a lunch, grab your fishing pole, and get away from it all at this 122-acre park on the Huron River, about seven miles from Ann Arbor. It's heavily wooded and boasts plenty of shady picnic areas, swings and slides, river fishing, and canoe launching. If you can get a team together, there's a baseball diamond here, too.

Introduce kids to nature at Dexter-Huron Metropark.
Photo courtesy of Huron-Clinton Metroparks

Dexter-Huron Metropark

Hours: 8am–10pm, Memorial Day–Labor Day; 8am–9am, rest of the year.

Cost: Daily $4 car permit, annual $20.

Directions: From I-94, take the Zeeb Road exit (#169), right on Zeeb, left on Huron River Drive.

Washtenaw County

Oakwoods Metropark

17845 Savage Road
Belleville, MI 48111
(734) 782-3956

A class participating in a special program at Oakwoods.
Photo courtesy of Huron-Clinton Metroparks

Oakwoods Metropark
Hours: 8am–dusk, seven days.
Cost: Daily vehicle entry permit, $2; weekends, $3.
Directions: From I-94, take the Haggerty Road exit (#192), left on Haggerty, right on Huron River Drive, left on Haggerty, continue on Savage Road.

This is one of the prettiest parks in the area, so much so that the views of the Huron River will make you forget that you're just a few minutes from traffic jams. It has all the amenities of other large metroparks in the area, but what sets Oakwoods apart is the cool nature center and the 700-foot, hard-surface trail that is ideal for baby strollers. Five miles of trails begin at the nature center, which features a turtle tank, snakes, frogs, toads, salamanders, and fish. There are nature-related programs held all year; call ahead for the schedule.

For Inquisitive Minds

Ann Arbor Hands-On Museum

220 E. Ann Street
Ann Arbor, MI 48104
(734) 995-1188
www.aahom.org

Ann Arbor Hands-On Museum
Hours: 10am–5pm, Mon–Sat; noon–5pm, Sun.
Cost: Children 2 or older, seniors and students $5; adults $7.
Directions: From M-14, take Main Street south to Ann Street, turn left.

Some of the men in my family refer to museums as the "M" word, mostly jokingly of course. Upon hearing the "M" word, kids might also conjure up images of a silent, austere, torturingly boring trap. But the Hands-On Museum will be a pleasant surprise for tots on up. After all, how many museums have you been to where shrieks of amazement and squeals of joy can be heard every few minutes?

Kids simply don't tire of visiting here—or parents, for that matter. Just a few blocks from the Kerrytown area, one of the state's oldest museums that caters to children of all ages, Hands-On is a place where learning is fun—sappy as that may sound.

Chapter Five

The Ann Arbor Hands-On Museum
Photo courtesy of Ann Arbor Area Convention and Visitors Bureau

One of the coolest, creepiest displays that still rattles me a little is a mirror you peer into as you pedal a stationary bicycle…Staring back at you is a skeleton riding a bike. There are oodles more exhibits in this section of the museum that focuses on bodies and how they work. Other sections include physics, nature, and light.

Opened in 1982 in the city's renovated red Central Fire House, the museum contains more than 250 exhibits. It offers special birthday party packages (I wonder if I'd get raised eyebrows if I had one for myself there), overnight camps, and special weekend workshops.

Make this a stop when you're in Ann Arbor—it should be on your "must do" list.

Cobblestone Farm Museum

2781 Packard Road
Ann Arbor, MI 48108
(734) 994-2928

Built in 1845, this charming farm showcases many examples of early Ann Arbor pioneering. The most interesting time to visit Cobblestone Farm is during the annual country Christmas programs,

> **Cobblestone Farm Museum**
>
> Hours: 1–4pm, Fri–Sun, or by appointment.
>
> Cost: Adults $2; seniors and children (3–17) $1.50; children under 3 free.
>
> Directions: From U.S. 23, take the Washtenaw Avenue exit (#37B), right on Washtenaw, left on Huron Parkway, continue on Platt Road, right on Packard.

when kids can join in traditional 1850s and 1860s holiday activities, like baking cookies in a wood stove and quilting. Autumn is fun, too, when visitors can help harvest crops and taste homemade apple butter.

Washtenaw County

Kempf House Center for Local History

312 S. Division Street
Ann Arbor, MI 48104
(734) 994-4898

Kempf House is an 1853 Greek Revival house that's been turned into a museum for interpreting Ann Arbor history and Victorian lifestyles from circa 1850 to 1910. You can tour the house, which is architecturally fantastic, but that might be dull for kids. They'll probably be more interested in participating in some of the special events hosted by Kempf House, like Christmas caroling through downtown with the Salvation Army Band, a German Family Christmas open house, and an annual Valentine's Day tea party. Call ahead for schedule.

The museum is named for Reuben and Pauline Kempf, prominent Ann Arbor musicians of the late-nineteenth and early-twentieth centuries.

> **Kempf House Center for Local History**
>
> Hours: Weekend and group tours by arrangement.
>
> Cost: Adults $1; children under 12 free.
>
> Directions: From M-14, take Main Street south to William Street, turn left, left on Division Street.

Museum of Natural History

University of Michigan
1109 Geddes Avenue
Ann Arbor, MI 48109
(734) 764-0478
www.exhibits.lsa.umich.edu/New/Welcome.html

Want at least a few almost guaranteed "oohs" and "ahhs" from the kids? Take them to see the state's largest collection of dinosaur skeletons. Displays explore Michigan's rich natural history with special focus on the prehistoric past. If you happen to be there on a weekend, check out one of the stargazing shows at the planetarium.

> **Museum of Natural History**
>
> Hours: 9am–5pm, Mon–Sat; noon–5pm, Sun.
>
> Cost: Free, but donation is suggested.
>
> Directions: From M-14, take Main Street south to Depot Street, turn left, right on Glen Avenue, left on Huron Street, continue on Washtenaw Avenue, right on Geddes.

Chapter Five

Kelsey Museum of Archeology

University of Michigan
434 S. State Street
Ann Arbor, MI 48109
(734) 764-9304

> **Kelsey Museum of Archeology**
>
> Directions: From M-14, take Main Street south to William Street, turn left, right on State.

The Kelsey Museum is home to a collection of about 100,000 objects from the civilizations of the Mediterranean. In an attempt to help kids ages 5–12 put their brains around the concept of such old stuff, family day programs bring the past alive through creative hands-on activities. Recent Egyptian family days featured a hieroglyph workshop, mummy making, crown and jewelry design. These special programs give kids the opportunity to learn about everyday people who lived in the ancient Egyptian, Greek, and Roman worlds.

U-M Museum of Art

525 S. State Street (at S. University Street)
Ann Arbor, MI 48109
(734) 764-0395

> **U-M Museum of Art**
>
> Hours: 10am–5pm, Tues–Sat; 10am–9 p.m, Thurs; noon–5pm, Sun; closed Mon.
>
> Cost: Free, but a $5 donation is suggested.
>
> Directions: From M-14, take Main Street south to William Street, turn left, right on State.

Contains nearly 17,000 works of art from throughout the world. Highlights include paintings by Picasso, Whistler, and Monet; photography by Ansel Adams; and a world-class collection of Asian art and antiques.

The museum often features family-friendly programs on weekends, including storytelling, concerts, and guided tours.

Charles Baird Carillon

Burton Memorial Tower
300 block of S. Thayer Street
University of Michigan campus
www.music.umich.edu/resources/facilities/carillon

> **Charles Baird Carillon**
>
> Directions: From M-14, take Main Street south to Washington, turn left, right on Thayer.

It's hard to miss this bell tower when you're on the U-M campus. Architect Albert Kahn designed Burton Memorial Tower in 1935. The ten-story structure is made of Indiana limestone. This is the third largest carillon in the world—and you might impress your kids by telling them that hammers sound the set of bells. The carillon is played on weekdays at noon and on most Saturday mornings. Guest musicians play recitals here on Monday evenings in June and July.

Check the website for special events and get a preview of the bells chiming.

Washtenaw County

Yankee Air Museum

801 Willow Run Airport
Ypsilanti, MI 48198
(734) 483-4030
www.yankeeairmuseum.org

Yankee Air Museum

Hours: 10am–4pm, Tues–Sat; noon–4pm, Sun; closed Mon & holidays.

Cost: Adults $7; children 5–12 $3; seniors and teens 13–19 $5.

Directions: Exit I-94 at the Willow Run Airport exit (#186), continue on Wiard Road, left on Airport Drive, right on Willow Run Airport.

My grandfather was a pilot and managed an airport, so I've been fascinated by airplanes since I was a kid. I think it's a safe assumption that most kids will be equally as intrigued by the display of interesting old aircraft usually seen only in movies or on old reruns of M.A.S.H.

Milestones of Southeastern Michigan aviation history, like the camouflage-painted Bell Huey UH-1 helicopter and numerous fighter planes, are on display in a historic hangar at Willow Run Airport. The hangar played a major role in producing close to 9,000 of the famous four-engine B-24 bombers during World War II. As you approach the vintage hangar, you have to pass an enormous eight-engine B-52 jet bomber with an intimidating snarl painted on its nose.

Willow Run is also host to many air shows throughout the year. They list other air shows in the state on their website.

Michigan Antique Fire Equipment Preservation Group

110 W. Cross Street
Ypsilanti, MI 48197
(734) 547-0663

Michigan Antique Fire Equipment Preservation Group

Hours: 2–5pm, first two Sundays of the month, or by appointment.

Cost: Free.

Directions: Exit I-94 at Huron Street (#183), right on Huron, left on Cross.

Lots of little boys (and maybe girls) go through fire truck fascination phases. This is a cool way to allow them an up-close view of these huge vehicles.

Housed in a beautiful brick fire station that was built in 1898, antique fire trucks, fire extinguishers, bells, helmets, poles, and photos that depict how fires were fought more than 100 years ago can be viewed.

Chapter Five

Ypsilanti Historical Museum

220 N. Huron Street
Ypsilanti, MI 48197
(734) 482-4990
www.ypsilantihistoricalmuseum.org

Ypsilanti Historical Museum

Hours: 2–4pm, Thurs, Sat, & Sun.

Cost: Free.

Directions: Exit I-94 at Huron Street (#183), right on Huron.

In this elegant, brick 1860 mansion you'll experience true Victorian style. Exhibit rooms showcase artifacts from nineteenth-century Ypsilanti, and kids may be most interested in the Toy Room. Here you'll be able to investigate what kids were playing way back in the day, like dolls, a toy piano, books, and a pair of ice skates made from wood and leather.

The museum hosts some fun events throughout the year, including a "trash and treasure" sale in June, a craft show in September, the Heritage Festival in August, and a Christmas open house.

Chelsea Depot Museum

125 Jackson Street
Chelsea, MI 48118
(734) 475-9330

Chelsea Depot Museum

Hours: 1–3pm, Sat.

Cost: Free.

Directions: Exit I-94 at Jackson Road (#162), right on Jackson, right on Main Street, right on Jackson Street.

Maintained by the Chelsea Area Historical Society, the Depot Museum still serves as the local Amtrak stop. Inside, you'll find railroad memorabilia, historical photos of Chelsea, and a pretty cool electric model-train display.

Chapter Six
Road Trips

If you're planning an extended stay in the state, you may want to explore the territory outside Southeastern Michigan. And for those of us who already live here, sometimes you just need a change of scenery.

Since we have friends and family all over the state, we spend a great deal of time on the road regardless of the weather. Listed here are options for trips that can be done in a day and some that are overnighters at least, probably even some that require weekend stays.

None should take you more than five hours from Metro Detroit, unless you encounter inclement weather or construction snarls. Since there are so many fun, interesting, and beautiful places in Michigan, this is just a small sampling of what the state has to offer.

Chapter Six

Within Two Hours

Brighton, MI

While there isn't a whole lot to downtown Brighton, it's very charming and is the perfect place to grab lunch in a little cafe before heading off to one of its huge recreation areas. Also, it's less than an hour away from most Metro Detroit suburbs.

> **Brighton, MI**
>
> Directions: north of Ann Arbor in Livingston County. To get to downtown Brighton from the east, take I-96 west to the Grand River Road Exit (#145), left on Grand River, right on Main Street.

Imagination Station

Located in the heart of downtown Brighton, the Imagination Station is a 10,000-square-foot playground. A series of wooden play structures create a fantasy, child-sized play area for kids of every age. While children explore the Imagination Station, adults can enjoy a stroll along the Millpond or tread on the new Tridge, a three-spiked bridge with an adjacent gazebo.

Brighton Recreation Area

With close to 5,000 acres, this massive park features several campgrounds, a number of lakes and ponds that are perfect for swimming and fishing, lots of terrain for cross-country skiers, and hills for sledders in the winter.

> **Brighton Recreation Area**
>
> Directions: Exit I-96 at the Brighton Exit (#147), head west about 6 miles to Chilson Road, then head south less than two miles to Bishop Lake Road.

Road Trips

Mt. Brighton Ski Area

4141 Bauer Road
Brighton, MI 48116
(810) 229-9581

Features about twenty-six runs at 250-feet vertical; the longest is 1,350 feet. It also has a restaurant named Bauery.

> **Mt. Brighton Ski Area**
>
> Directions: Exit I-96 at Grand River Avenue (#145), left on Grand River, right on Challis, left on Bauer.

Irish Hills

Located along U.S. 12 near Coldwater

Legend has it that the region was named by an Irish immigrant minister for its resemblance to his native country. The area has long been a vacation spot for families, with lots of quirky places within a few miles of one another.

> **Irish Hills**
>
> Directions: Located along U.S. 12 near Coldwater. From Ann Arbor, take I-94 to U.S. 127, south on U.S. 127 to State Route 50 to U.S. 12.

Prehistoric Forest, Jungle Rapids Water Slide and Mystery Hill

8203 U.S. 12
Onstead, MI 49265
(517) 467-2514

This complex of kitschy entertainment combines depictions of life-size dinosaurs, splashy water fun, and a stream that appears to be running up a hill. There are go-carts, batting cages, and a plethora of other activities. Combo tickets can be purchased for all three places.

> **Prehistoric Forest, Jungle Rapids Water Slide and Mystery Hill**
>
> Directions: From U.S. 12, take the Saline exit (#34), right on Michigan Avenue, continue on U.S. 12.

Chapter Six

Stagecoach Stop U.S.A.

7203 U.S. 12
Onsted, MI 49265
(517) 467-2300

This frontier town resembles what a Michigan city what have been like in the 1800s. It features a general store, petting zoo, and amphitheater that seats about 2,000 for summer concerts.

> **Stagecoach Stop U.S.A.**
>
> Directions: From U.S. 12, take the Saline exit (#34), right on Michigan Avenue, continue on U.S. 12.

Hayes State Park

Entrance is on U.S. 12 near Michigan 124 in Onsted
(517) 467-7401

Campgrounds, swimming, fishing, and boating.

Brooklyn

Michigan International Speedway

11522 Brooklyn Rd.
(517) 592-2114

Stock and Indy-style cars race on a D-shaped track most summer weekends.

> **Michigan International Speedway**
>
> Directions: From U.S. 12, exit at Saline (#34), right on Michigan Avenue, right on M-50, left on Daugherty Road, right on Brooklyn.

Road Trips

East Lansing

Home to Michigan State University, East Lansing has a host of things for families to do. Try to make a day of shopping at some of the funky boutiques and MSU-logo stores along Grand River Avenue, then stay for dinner.

> **East Lansing**
>
> Directions: From the Detroit area, take I-96 to I-496 north and follow the signs to downtown or the main campus exit, Trowbridge Road.

Michigan State University

The beautiful 5,200-acre MSU campus lends itself to walks with the kids—especially if you're visiting in the fall when the leaves are changing color and the air is crisp. The Red Cedar River flows between campus buildings and there are plenty of benches for resting.

MSU Children's Garden

On Bogue Street, behind the Plant and Soil Science Building, adjacent to the Horticulture Gardens (517) 355-0348

Visit the "Pizza Garden," a garden shaped like its namesake that features all the herbs that make a delicious pie and sixty-or-so themed gardens with a sense of humor.

Chapter Six

MSU Dairy Store

Center of campus on Farm Lane
(517) 355-8466

Have an ice cream cone and take home some cheese—all products come from the MSU dairy barns.

Butterfly House

MSU campus, in the teaching greenhouses
at the corner of Bogue and Wilson
(517) 355-0348

Walk through and witness hundreds of species of butterflies. Best visited in the summer, when the lovely creatures are more active.

Bug House

MSU campus in the Natural Science Building
(517) 355-4662

No, this is not a dorm room gone awry. The Bug House showcases hundreds of creepy, crawly insects from all over the United States and the world.

Beaumont Tower

MSU campus, near the museum

The forty-nine-bell carillon is home to free weekly concerts in the summer.

Road Trips

MSU Museum

MSU campus on West Circle Drive
(517) 355-2370

Three floors of Michigan history and artifacts, with a great gift shop.

Kresge Art Museum

MSU campus, at the intersection of Auditorium and Physics Road
(517) 355-7631

Great permanent collection, including the works of Andy Warhol, Salvador Dali, and architect Louis Sullivan.

Wharton Center for the Performing Arts

MSU campus, at the corner of Center and Wharton
(517) 432-2000

Two auditoriums feature year-round concerts and theatrical performances. Kids might enjoy the free backstage tours that are given on Sundays. Call for times.

Abrams Planetarium

MSU Campus, at the corner of Science Road and Shaw Lane
(517) 355-4672

Special family shows on Sundays. Call for schedule.

Chapter Six

Fenton

Balloon Quest Inc.:
Captain Phogg Balloon Rides
2470 Grange Hall Road
Fenton, MI 48430

Every now and then if you're cruising along I-75, you'll be surprised by one of these brightly colored hot air balloons taking off. The hour-long rides are probably best for older kids and brave adults. Gift certificates and group rates are available.

> **Balloon Quest Inc.:**
> **Captain Phogg Balloon Rides**
>
> Directions: From Metro Detroit, expect the drive to be about an hour. Exit I-75 at Grange Hall Road (#101), left on Grange Hall.

Flint

Located near the intersection of I-75, U.S. Highway 23, and Interstate 69, Flint is very much a "drive past" city for many people who travel the state. There are, however, some real family-friendly gems here. For even more information, contact the Flint Area Convention and Visitors Bureau, (800) 232-8900, or at www.flint.org.

Flint Institute of Arts
1120 E. Kearsley
Flint, MI 48503
(810) 234-1695

Permanent collection of nearly 5,000 works of art from the eighteenth century forward. The museum hosts special events including art fairs. They also have a nice gift shop.

> **Flint Institute of Arts**
>
> Directions: Exit I-475 at Downtown Flint (#111), take the Court Street exit (#7), continue on northbound Chavez Drive, right on Kearsley.

Road Trips

Robert T. Longway Planetarium

1310 E. Kearsley
Flint, MI 48503
(810) 760-1181
www.longwayplanetarium.com

Robert T. Longway Planetarium
Directions: Exit I-475 at Downtown Flint (#111), take the Court Street exit (#7), continue on northbound Chavez Drive, right on Kearsley.

The Robert T. Longway Planetarium, Michigan's largest, features 285 seats under a sixty-foot dome. It's Learning Center has hands-on science demonstrations, telescope workshops, and astronomy lessons for children.

Flint Children's Museum

1602 W. Third Avenue
Flint, MI 48504
(810) 767-5437

Flint Children's Museum
Directions: Exit I-75 at I-69 (#117A), take the Hammerberg Road exit (#135), left on Hammerberg, right on M-21/Court Street, left on Chevrolet Avenue, right on Third.

Hands-on learning and entertainment featuring exhibits related to technology and science.

Historic Crossroads Village and Huckleberry Railroad

G-6140 Bray Road
Flint, MI 48506
(800) 648-7272

Historic Crossroads Village and Huckleberry Railroad
Directions: Exit I-475 at Downtown Flint (#111), take the Stewart Avenue/Dort Highway exit (#9), right on Carpenter Road, left on Bray.

The history of the 1800s in Michigan comes to life at this attraction next to Mott Lake. You'll find everything from a steam train ride through the countryside—complete with a visit by faux robbers every hour—to a look of what the Flint area was like in the "olden days," as my eight-year-old stepdaughter refers to anything older than she is.

Chapter Six

Birch Run

Years ago, this was a farming community. Now, it's a farming community with a gigantic outlet mall and some other worthwhile attractions. You can see it from I-75, just a breeze north of Flint.

Prime Outlets

12240 S. Beyer Road
Birch Run, MI 48415
(989) 624-4868

> **Prime Outlets**
>
> Directions: Exit I-75 at Exit #136, left on Birch Run Road, left on Beyer.

This is one of the only deviations from my "no chain" rule for this book. I find it worthy of straying from the rule because it's a nice mall with lots of kids' play areas to help keep them occupied while parents shop. Plus, it's not contained to one large structure; you actually have to walk outside to get from store to store, which is a rare treat in mall environments. It has more than 170 stores.

Wilderness Trails Animal Park

11721 Gera Road (M-83)
Birch Run, MI 48415
(989) 624-6177

> **Wilderness Trails Animal Park**
>
> Directions: Exit I-75 at Exit #136, right on Birch Run Road, left on Gera.

When my mother worked for the Saginaw Public School System, this was a favorite field trip for the little ones. This fifty-six-acre park has more than sixty species of exotic animals including foxes, cougars, bears, buffalo, and monkeys.

Road Trips

Tony's Restaurant

8781 Main Street
Birch Run, MI 48415
(989) 624-5860

Tony's Restaurant
Directions: Exit I-75 at Exit #136, left on
Birch Run Road (Main Street).

Mid-Michigan residents are very well versed in the Tony's dining experience—portions that two people can easily share and very low prices. Start the diet Monday and add a milkshake to your order of a burger and fries. Your kids will delight in ordering what is perhaps the most alarmingly huge banana split I've ever seen.

"Let's go to Tony's Restaurant!" Photo by Howard Lovy

Chapter Six

Frankenmuth

This is a kitsch-heavy but very family-oriented village east of Birch Run. Upon arrival, you're sure to think you've stepped into a Little Bavaria, and that's OK with the folks in Frankenmuth. Stop by on your way to Northern Michigan, or make a weekend trip out of it—I know many Southeastern Michigan families who plan entire vacations around this town. The following is just a touch of what you'll find here.

Bronner's Christmas Wonderland

25 Christmas Lane
Frankenmuth, MI 48734
(800) ALL-YEAR
www.bronners.com

Bronner's Christmas Wonderland

Directions: Exit I-75 at Exit #136, right on Birch Run Road, left on Gera Road, right on Weiss Street, left on Christmas Lane.

It's always Christmas at Bronner's, one of the largest stores of its kind. Photo courtesy of Frankenmuth Convention and Visitors Bureau

They claim to be the world's largest Christmas store, and they're probably right. From larger-than-life mechanical figures to the tiniest handmade ornaments, if it's Christmas-related, it'll be for sale at Bronner's. I even found some Hanukkah stuff for my husband here. It's more than just shopping; it's an experience, no matter what your cultural lot is.

A Parent's Guide to
Southeastern Michigan

Road Trips

Bavarian Inn

713 S. Main Street
Frankenmuth, MI 48734
(800) 652-9941

> **Bavarian Inn**
>
> Hours: 11am–9pm, seven days.
>
> Directions: Exit I-75 at Exit #136, right on Birch Run Road, left on Gera Road, which turns into Main Street.

Famous for its all-you-can-eat chicken dinners. While you're here, check out the Glockenspiel Tower, a thirty-five–bell carillon imported from Germany. The restaurant is affiliated with the Bavarian Inn Lodge, an enormous hotel with five indoor pools, an eighteen-hole indoor miniature golf course, and a special children's village. Call (888) 775-6343 for more info.

The Bavarian Inn hosts lots of family-friendly activities throughout the year. Photo courtesy of Frankenmuth Convention and Visitors Bureau

Chapter Six

Zehnder's

730 S. Main Street
Frankenmuth, MI 48734
(800) 863-7999

Zehnder's

Hours: 11am–9:30pm, daily.

Directions: Exit I-75 at Exit #136, right on Birch Run Road, left on Gera Road, which turns into Main Street.

Another all-you-can-eat chicken dinner empire. In addition to the restaurant, Zehnder's features an eighteen-hole championship golf course, a hotel, and shops. Also hosts "Snowfest," an outside winter carnival every February.

Pretzels are a traditional Bavarian treat.
Photo courtesy of Frankenmuth Convention and Visitors Bureau

Road Trips

Bridgeport

Junction Valley Railroad

7065 Dixie Highway
Bridgeport, MI 48722
(989) 777-3480

Located just north of Frankenmuth along I-75, Junction Valley features a two-mile ride through the woods in a miniature train. There is also a picnic area and a playground.

> **Junction Valley Railroad**
>
> Hours: Open 10am–6pm, Mon–Sat, 1pm–6 m, Sun. Memorial Day–Labor Day.
>
> Cost: $4.25, children 2–12; $5 adults and seniors.
>
> Directions: Exit I-75 at Birch Run/Frankenmuth (#136), left on Birch Run Road, right on Maple Road, left on Dixie Highway.

Saginaw

Japanese Cultural Center and Tea House

527 Ezra Rust Drive
Saginaw, MI 48602
(989) 759-1648

Pretty little spot near the Saginaw River often used for weddings. The teahouse is of authentic design and hosts traditional tea ceremonies. Offers interesting classes such as origami, bonsai, and calligraphy. Call for more information.

> **Japanese Cultural Center and Tea House**
>
> Hours: Call for hours and special class times.
>
> Directions: Exit I-75 at #149, right on Holland Road, right on Remington Street, left on Sheridan Avenue, right on Rust Street, right on Washington Avenue, left on Ezra Rust Drive.

Chapter Six

Anderson Water Park

1860 Fordney Street
Saginaw, MI 48602
(989) 759-1386

Two water slides, wave pool, sunbathing area, and a concession stand.

Anderson Water Park
Call for seasonal hours and admission.
Directions: Exit I-75 at Dixie Highway (#144B), left on Williamson, right on Fordney.

Bay City

St. Laurent Brothers Nut House

1101 N. Water Street
Bay City, MI 48708
(989) 893-7522

Funny name, but awesome fresh nuts. This place is known far and wide for its selection of delectable legumes, chocolates, and candies. If your kids have a sweet tooth, it's worth the trip.

St. Laurent Brothers Nut House
Hours: 9am–9pm, Mon–Sat; 11am–5pm, Sun.
Directions: Exit I-75 at M-25 east toward downtown Bay City (#162A), left on Water Street.

Bay City State Recreation Area

3582 State Park Drive
Bay City, MI 48706
(989) 684-3020

Situated pleasantly on the Saginaw Bay, this state park offers five mile of trails, more than 260 campsites, swimming, and all sorts of winter sports.

Bay City State Recreation Area
Hours: Day-use visitors, dawn–dusk.
Cost: Camp sites $13–$15 per night.
Directions: Exit I-75 at Beaver Road (#168), travel east 5 miles to the park.

Road Trips

Midland

Located north of Saginaw and west of Bay City, Midland has a pleasant, compact downtown area that runs along the Tittabawassee River. If you stop here with the kids, be sure to check out the "Tridge," an interesting, three-cornered bridge located near the corner of Main and Ashman Streets.

Midland Center for the Arts

1801 W. St. Andrews Road
Midland, MI 48640
(989) 631-5930
www.mcfta.org

The section here that will entertain children for hours is called the Hall of Ideas, which features four levels of exciting and unique interactive exhibits. The center runs a family series of performances in its auditorium each fall and hosts two juried art fairs.

Midland Center for the Arts

Hours: 10am–6pm daily.

Cost: $2, children under 12; $4 adults.

Directions: Exit I-75 at U.S. 10 west toward Midland (#162B), take the M-20 exit toward downtown Midland, continue on M-20, which becomes Eastman, the center is at Eastman and St. Andrews.

Dow Gardens

1018 W. Main Street
Midland, MI 48640
(800) 362-4874
www.dowgardens.org

This is probably one of the most pleasant places in mid-Michigan for an afternoon walk. More than 100 acres are teaming with identified trees, shrubs, herbaceous perennials, and flowers. The most exciting time of the year for kids to visit Dow Gardens is between March and April for "Butterflies in Bloom," when the conservatory comes alive with hundreds of colorful butterflies.

Dow Gardens

Hours: Year-round, 9am–one hour before sunset; closed holidays.

Cost: $5 adults, $1 for kids 6–17.

Directions: Exit I-75 at U.S.-10 west (#162B) toward Midland, take the M-20 exit toward downtown Midland, left on McDonald Street, right on Larkin Street, left on Hubbard Street, right on Main.

Chapter Six

Chippewa Nature Center

400 S. Badour Road
Midland, MI 48640
(989) 631-0830
www.chippewanaturecenter.com

More than 1,000 acres and fourteen miles of trails through woods, fields, rivers, and wetlands. The visitor center showcases a gallery, wildlife viewing-area classrooms, and an auditorium. A fun family event held each March is the "Maple Sugaring Weekend," which allows visitors to watch the entire process of making syrup.

Chippewa Nature Center

Hours and Cost: Grounds are open daily and are free; call or see website for info on special events.

Directions: Exit I-75 at U.S. 10 west (#162B) toward Midland, take M-20 west toward downtown Midland, left on Cronkright Street, bear right on Poseyville Road, right on River Street, right on Towsley Street, right on Whitman Drive, bear left on Atwell Street, right on Pine River Road, right on Badour.

Pere Marquette Rail Trail

Entrances in downtown Midland near the Tridge and at various city parks
(989) 832-6874

Maintained, in part by the Midland County Parks and Recreation Department, this thirty-mile paved trail is a good example of recycling railroad tracks that are no longer in use. Depending on your stamina, the section of the trail that runs from Sanford to Coleman crosses three former railroad bridges that afford terrific views. Perfect for in-line skating, biking, running, or walking.

Road Trips

Northern Michigan

Traverse City

At the intersections of U.S. 31 and M-72

With more waterfront resorts, hotels, and campsites than you can shake a cherry tree at (the area is one of the largest producers of cherries in the U.S.),

Traverse City

Directions: From Metro Detroit, take I-75 about 190 miles to M-72 (exit #254 toward Grayling). Stay on M-72 through Grayling and Kalkaska. Make a left on U.S. 31 when you reach Lake Michigan. The drive is a little more than 4 hours.

Traverse City has become the place to vacation for Michiganians. It's such a pleasant retreat that my grandparents even honeymooned here years ago. The downtown area is walkable and pleasant and offers many restaurant choices. No matter where you are downtown, you're never too far from a spectacular view of the East or West Grand Traverse bays of Lake Michigan.

A view of Lake Michigan. Photo by Howard Lovy

Chapter Six

Old Mission Peninsula Lighthouse

**On M-37, bisecting the east and
west arms of Grand Traverse Bay**

The kids will get a kick out of standing
halfway between the equator and the North Pole
at this lighthouse situated on the forty-fifth paral-
lel. The actual lighthouse is rather small, with a
tower of about thirty feet and the inside is closed to the public. It's worth a trip
for the beach, which has an unusually slow drop off and provides lots of shallow
water for little ones.

Old Mission Peninsula Lighthouse

Directions: From U.S. 31, take M-37
north about seven miles to the tip
of Old Mission Peninsula.

Clinch Park

This clean, easily accessible public beach gets
crowded in the summer, but children have fun
making new friends and constructing sandcastles
with each other on the shore of Lake Michigan.
Lifeguards are on duty seasonally.

Clinch Park

Directions: In downtown Traverse
City on U.S. 31 at Cass. Follow U.S.
31 around the Bay when coming
from the south.

Clinch Park Zoo

**In downtown Traverse City on Grandview Parkway,
right next to the beach
(231) 922-4904**

This quaint, manageable-sized zoo features wildlife native to the state, such as
black bears, elk, and otters. The otters are so hilarious to watch that you might
actually have to drag the kids away from the exhibit. Don't leave without at least
one spin around the zoo on the small steam train.

Road Trips

Dennos Museum Center

Northwestern Michigan College
1701 E. Front Street
Traverse City, MI 49686
www.nmc.edu/~dennos
(231) 922-1055

> **Dennos Museum Center**
>
> Hours: 10am–5pm, Mon–Sat;
> 1–5pm, Sun
>
> Cost: $4 adults, $2 kids
>
> Directions: From U.S 31, turn right on Davis Street, left on Indian Woods Drive, right on Front Street.

The permanent Inuit Art Gallery is spectacular, with more than 500 pieces depicting the harsh life and fascinating culture of these Arctic people. What'll interest the kids, however, is Discovery Gallery, a mammoth section combining art, science, and technology into intriguing hands-on exhibits. This is a nice place to keep in mind if it rains all over your camping trip—although it's cool enough to make a trip regardless of the weather.

Interlochen

Fun Country Amusement Park

9320 U.S. 31 South
Interlochen, MI 49643
(231) 276-6360

> **Fun Country Amusement Park**
>
> Directions: From Traverse City, take U.S. 31 south.

Waterslide park with go-carts, miniature golf, bumper boats, a merry-go-round, a train, and food concessions.

Chapter Six

Interlochen Center for the Arts

On Michigan 137, south of the U.S. 31 intersection
(231) 276-6230
www.interlochen.org

Interlochen Center for the Arts

Directions: On Michigan 137, south of the U.S. 31 intersection. From Traverse City, take U.S. 31 south to M-137, turn left.

The beautiful campus includes a world-renowned arts academy (one famous alum is singer Jewel), arts camp, and arts festival that annually produces more than 700 concerts, plays, readings, and exhibits by students and teachers. Also, it is home to the area's only National Public Radio affiliate station. National music acts play in the covered outdoor Kresge Auditorium throughout the summer.

Interlochen State Park

(231) 276-9511

Interlochen State Park

Directions: One mile south of U.S. 31 on Michigan 137. From Traverse City, take U.S. 31 south.

The park has about 500 campsites on both Duck Lake and Green Lake, near the Interlochen Center for the Arts. It also features beaches, a bathhouse, and boat rentals.

Road Trips

Empire

Sleeping Bear Dunes Climb
Off M-109, eight miles north of Empire

Energetic people of all ages love the knee-bending climb up this towering, 150-foot sand dune, or more likely, they love the exhilarating run back down. The reward—other than getting your heart rate up a bit—is a spectacular view of Glen Lake at the dunes' summit.

> **Sleeping Bear Dunes Climb**
>
> Directions: From Traverse City, take M-72 west to M-109, turn right. Off M-109, 8 miles north of Empire.

Sarah enjoys the view from a high spot at the Sleeping Bear Dunes Climb. Photo by Howard Lovy

Chapter Six

Pierce Stocking Scenic Drive
**Located off M-109 south of
the Sleeping Bear Dunes Climb
(231) 326-5134**

Located off M-109 south of the Sleeping
Bear Dunes Climb. Pick up a self-guided tour
brochure at the entrance and have one of the

Pierce Stocking Scenic Drive

Directions: From Traverse City, take
M-72 west to M-109, turn right.

kids narrate each scenic stop. The drive takes you through more than seven miles
of dunes and woods providing breathtaking scenery, including views of Lake
Michigan. Two picnic areas with restrooms are available.

Leelanau Peninsula

Often referred to as the "Little Finger" of Michigan, the rolling hills, cherry
tree orchards, and Lake Michigan shorelines of the Leelanau Peninsula make a
favorite vacation spot for many. It also happens to be where my parents now
reside, lucky for us! It's accessible via M-22, which runs in a loop around the
peninsula. Drive about twenty minutes north of Traverse City for a day trip, or
spend a week exploring the quaint villages, vigorous hiking trails, and pristine
beaches that make up the peninsula. Following are some of our favorite stomping
grounds in Leelanau, which is the Native American word for "the land of
delight." See www.leelanau.com for more info.

Sonya's kite gets some air on the beach at Lake Michigan. Photo by Howard Lovy

Road Trips

Leland

This small town along scenic M-22 could easily be mistaken for a small New England village—quaint, charming, and picturesque. You'll find plenty of good restaurants, great shopping, and one of the prettiest marinas we've ever seen here.

Fishtown

Near Leland's marina, these rows of historic wooden "shanties" were restored and converted. It now houses unique stores and great places to buy smoked fish.

Leland's Fishtown. Photo by Beth Ann Young

Chapter Six

North and South Manitou Islands
(231) 256-9061

Pack up your camping equipment and head out to North or South Manitou for a rustic adventure. South Manitou has three camping areas, but North Manitou is "open," meaning you just pick a spot anywhere on the 15,000 acres. Guided tours and day trips are available, too. Frequent departures from Manitou Island Transit at the end of Fishtown. Call for times and ticket information.

Northport

Leelanau State Park
15310 N. Lighthouse Point Road
Northport, MI 49670
(231) 386-5422

Leelanau State Park

Directions: From Traverse City, take M-22 north to the very tip of the Leelanau Peninsula.

The 800-acre Leelanau State Park sits at the very tip of Leelanau Peninsula on Lake Michigan amid coastal dunes and beaches where it's fun to look for Petoskey stones (a fossil that is the Michigan state stone) with the kids. Choose from any of the fifty rustic campsites and be sure to check out Grand Traverse Lighthouse, which was built in 1852 and is now a museum.

An 8.5-mile hiking and skiing trail meanders through the park and has spurs leading to views of Cathead Bay and to the beach.

Annual Dog Parade
Downtown Northport
www.leelanau.com/northport

Held every August, this pooch prance is a dog lovers' delight. Dozens of locals deck their canine pals out in costumes centering on a theme ("Harry Potter," etc.) and trek down the center of town. Check www.leelanau.com/northport for dates.

Road Trips

Peterson Park

Peterson Park

Directions: From Traverse City, take M-22 north. The park is about a mile north of downtown Northport off M-22; watch for the sign—it sneaks up on you on the left when you're headed north.

Situated high on the bluffs of Lake Michigan, Peterson Park might just win the "Most Perfect Picnic Spot" in the entire state—at the least, it's a popular spot for watching the sunset over the lake. If you're feeling ambitious, venture down the long railroad tie staircase and look for pretty stones to take home; but don't forget you have to make the steep climb back up. There is a volleyball area and playscape to keep the kids occupied while the grownups swoon over the views of the Manitou and Fox Islands.

Suttons Bay

Home to the Leelanau Peninsula's only movie theater, Suttons Bay maintains its village charm while offering amenities not easily found in other nearby areas. Hansen's Grocery Store sells gourmet fare and fresh vegetables to rival any big city market and the vegetarian Cafe Bliss is always serving something delightful. Down the hill, a park near Suttons Bay Marina has a nice playscape for kids and is host to a long-running juried art fair every August. If you visit the fair, that's my father and his cohorts serving the traditional pancake breakfast on Sunday morning (proceeds benefit a different charitable cause each year).

Lima Bean
222 Saint Joseph
Suttons Bay, MI 49682
(231) 271-5462

Cool boutique that carries lots of original gift-type items for kids and fabulous clothing for women.

Chapter Six

Enerdyne

223 Saint Joseph
Suttons Bay, MI 49682
(231) 271-6033
www.enerdynet.com

A fun and educational store for kids with a focus on science and nature.

45th Parallel Cafe

102 S. Broadway Street
Suttons Bay, MI 49682
(231) 271-2233

A cute little cafe right in the center of town. Great breakfast spot—especially if you can get a seat on the patio out front.

Black Star Farms

10844 E. Revold Road
Suttons Bay, MI 49682
(231) 271-4970
www.blackstarfarms.com

You can't miss this enormous, rambling red estate as you drive north up M-22 from Traverse City. It houses a winery, a B & B and is home to some of the best cheese

Black Star Farms

Directions: From Traverse City, take M-22 north to Revold Road, turn left.

ever. Friends of our family Anne and John Hoyt own Leelanau Cheese, makers of excellent traditional European-style cheeses. Stop by and watch them create!

Road Trips

Glen Arbor

This is a beautiful little downtown area situated along M-22 right on Lake Michigan. There are plenty of restaurants, cafes, galleries, and boutiques to warrant a weekend stay here, but you can also just stop for a few hours for a sampling. My husband and I are a tad partial to the town, since we chose a spot here for our 2001 wedding.

Cherry Republic

6026 Lake Street
Glen Arbor, MI 49636
(800) 206-6949
www.cherryrepublic.com

Cherry Republic

Directions: From Traverse City, take M-72 west to M-22, turn right.

Nothing says Northern Michigan more than a yummy cherry treat, and you'll find just about every concoction possible here. Sample dark chocolate-covered cherries, cherry/nut mixes, and even cherry salsa then decide what you want to take home. We even had cherry truffles made here for our wedding favors. Since you can sample pretty much everything they make, keep an eye on the kids or you're sure to have some upset tummies later from overindulging.

Chapter Six

Cottage Book Shop

5989 Lake Street
Glen Arbor, MI 49636
(231) 334-4223
www.cottagebooks.com

An adorable log cabin that houses very thoughtful shelves of books for kids and adults.

Cottage Book Shop

Directions: From Traverse City, take M-72 west to M-22, turn right. Once you're in downtown Glen Arbor, turn right on Lake Street.

Crystal River Canoe Livery

6249 Western Avenue (M-22)
Glen Arbor, MI 49636
(231) 334-4420

Rent a canoe or kayak and spend the afternoon traversing this picturesque, seven-mile river. They say the journey should take no longer than two and a half hours, but if you're as uncoordinated as we are, plan an entire afternoon around it. Dragonflies abound.

Crystal River Canoe Livery

Directions: From Traverse City, take M-72 west to M-22, turn right.

Road Trips

Western Michigan

Battle Creek

Kellogg's Cereal City U.S.A.

171 W. Michigan Avenue
Battle Creek, MI 49017
(800) 970-7020
www.kelloggscerealcityusa.org

Long the home to cereal makers Kellogg, Ralston, and Post, manufacturers stopped factory tours years ago. Now, you can check out this museum that explores cereal from the field to the flakes in your bowl. There are plenty of hands-on activities for kids and theater presentations. Call ahead or check the website for special breakfast-with-"Tony the Tiger" days.

Holland

This city was settled by the Dutch in the nineteenth century, hence the name. Many customs remain today and can be witnessed in full force annually at the Tulip Time Festival in May. The festival features about eight miles of blooming tulips, a parade, and other family-friendly activities.

Kellogg's Cereal City U.S.A.

Hours: 10am–5pm, Fri–Sat; noon–5pm, Sun, in winter; call for summer hours.

Cost: Adults $7.95; kids 3-12 $4.95; seniors $6.50; kids under 2 free.

Directions: From Metro Detroit, take I-94 across the state, exit at #104 in Battle Creek, which will put you on Michigan Avenue. Kellogg is less than five miles from the highway. The drive is a little over two hours.

Holland

Directions: Located about 30 miles east of Grand Rapids. From Metro Detroit it's about a 3 hour drive. Take I-94 west until Kalamazoo, then take U.S. 131 north to Allegan, from there take M-89 through Hamilton where it becomes M-40. Take M-40 into downtown Holland.

Chapter Six

Windmill Island

Downtown Holland at Seventh Street and Lincoln Avenue
(616) 355-1030

Visit the miniature Dutch village for dancing demonstrations and guided tours during the summer. In order to get to the 200-year-old working windmill, you'll have to cross an authentic Dutch drawbridge.

Dutch Village

Downtown Holland at James Street and U.S. 31
(800) 285-7177

Wooden shoe carvers, imported gifts, and folk dancing are displayed amid Dutch gardens and architecture.

Grand Haven

Musical Fountain

Children love to watch this musical fountain "perform"—jets of water are choreographed to music and lights and spew streams up to 125 feet in the air. Free grandstand seating accommodates about 2,500.

> **Musical Fountain**
>
> Shows nightly Memorial Day–Labor Day.
>
> Directions: On the river in downtown Grand Haven. From Holland, take U.S. 31 north.

Mackinaw Kite and Toy Company

106 Washington Street
Grand Haven, MI 49417
(800) 622-4655
www.mackite.com

With more than 100 types of kites, you're sure to find something to suit the needs and whims of everyone in the family.

> **Mackinaw Kite and Toy Company**
>
> Hours: 10am–8pm, Mon–Fri, 10am–6pm, Sat, closed Sun.
>
> Directions: From Holland, take U.S. 31 north, turn left on Franklin Avenue, right on First Street, store is at the corner of Washington and First.

Road Trips

Muskegon

Michigan's Adventure Amusement Park

4750 Whitehall Road (U.S. 31)
Muskegon, MI 49455
(231) 766-3377
www.miadventure.com

The state's largest amusement park boasts five wooden roller coasters and a bunch of tamer rides for the little ones. The park is combined with Wild Water Adventure, the state's largest water park.

> **Michigan's Adventure Amusement Park**
>
> Hours: 11am–9pm, all summer; call ahead, times subject to change.
>
> Cost: $23 for all ages, children under 2 free; season passes are available for $90 per person.
>
> Directions: Take I-96 west across the state, past Grand Rapids, take U.S. 31 north and exit at Ludington (#1B), take the Russell Road exit and turn left, right on Tyler Road, right on Whitehall Road. About three hours from the Metro Detroit area.

Out of State

Cedar Point Amusement Park

One Cedar Point Drive
Sandusky, Ohio 44870
www.cedarpoint.com

If you've grown up in Michigan, odds are your first introduction to a roller coaster was at Cedar Point. It's the biggest and best amusement park in the region that caters to adventure seekers of all

> **Cedar Point Amusement Park**
>
> Directions: The drive should take just a little over 2 hours from the Detroit area and it's pretty much a straight shot out of Michigan south on I-75 and a jaunt east on the Ohio turnpike. The website has excellent directions and a link to maps.

ages. They usually introduce a new coaster every year, the most recent of which is the "Top Thrill Dragster," debuting to those crazy enough to hop on it for the 2003 season. It has a 420-foot drop and reaches speeds of 120 miles per hour.

Chapter Six

Point Pelee National Park

407 Robson Street, R. R. #1
Leamington, Ontario, Canada N8H3V
(519) 322-2365
www.canadaparks.com

This national park that juts out into Lake Erie at the southernmost point of Canada features hiking, bird watching, beaches, cross-country skiing, and canoeing. It's about forty-five minutes from the Detroit-Windsor border.

Pelee Island

Tourism info: (519) 724-2931

This 10,000-acre island is home to about 300 permanent residents and about 1,000 people who maintain summer cottages. Highlights include beaches, camping, and the Pelee Lighthouse, which was built in 1833 and restored in 2000. Ferry service to the island from Ontario is continuous from mid-March to mid-December.

Point Pelee National Park

Hours: Change seasonally; 6am–9:30pm, all summer.

Cost: Adults $3.25, seniors $2.40, kids 6-16 $1.60, kids under 6 free. Annual passes are also available (Prices are in Canadian currency, park attendants will do American exchange.)

Directions: Drive is about an hour from the Detroit-Windsor Tunnel. From the tunnel, turn left on Ouellette Avenue, travel south on Ouellette and veer right at Howard Avenue and continue south to the third set of lights, turn left on Highway #3, follow signs to park entrance.

Pelee Island

Directions: Takes about an hour from the Detroit-Windsor border. Take the Ambassador Bridge to Canada (don't forget your passport), which will take you directly to Highway 3 east. Exit at Division Road and turn right. Once you're in Kingsville, the green and white signs will guide you to the ferry dock.

Appendices

Calendar of Regional Events

From over-the-top car-related events to enough art fairs to placate even the most discerning collector, you'll find events in Southeastern Michigan and beyond sure to entertain, educate, and inspire the entire family.

In the following pages are highlighted events for each month of the year. Have an itch for kitsch? Check out the Michigan Elvis Festival. In the mood for motion? Choose from racing yachts or hot air balloons. With such a tremendous variety of annual events and festivals, it's relatively simple to find a unique way to hang out with the family for the day.

Car buffs won't want to miss Autorama, the Woodward Avenue Dream Cruise, or the North American International Auto Show. Braving winter weather is worthwhile at the Plymouth International Ice Sculpture Spectacular, the Wayne County Lightfest, and the New Year Jubilee of Southeastern Michigan.

Cultural diversity is also at the forefront of a variety of statewide events. Check out the African World Festival, Fiesta Mexicana, and the Arab and Chaldean Festival—the largest event of its kind held in the United States.

For additional events and last minute planning, I've found two local newspapers, *Metro Times* and *Metro Parent*, to be invaluable resources (see page 13 for how to get your hands on a paper). Also, check out key websites for local events hosted by the Detroit Metro Convention and Visitor's Bureau and the state of Michigan (see page 14 for more info).

Appendix

January

North American International Auto Show

The Motor City hosts the annual North American International Auto Show. Photo by Vito Palmisano

Check out the latest and greatest cars during this annual ten-day extravaganza at Cobo Conference and Exhibition Center in Detroit. See **www.naias.com** for info, dates, and tickets. Tickets also can be purchased through TicketMaster.

Plymouth International Ice Sculpture Spectacular

Skilled ice carvers from across the U.S. and Canada, and from as far away as Japan, brave the frigid Michigan winter to create their beautiful works and displays. Admission is free, and the displays can be viewed twenty-four hours. (734) 459-9157.

Ann Arbor Folk Festival

An annual tradition since 1977 featuring acoustic music. (734) 761-1800.

Calendar

February

Detroit Boat Show

Boats of every size imaginable at Cobo Exhibition and Conference Center. For information call (734) 261-0123.

Autorama

Hot rods, muscle cars, and custom cars galore at Cobo Conference and Exhibition Center in Detroit. Your family should be true car fanatics to attend. (248) 293-1700.

March

Detroit Kennel Club Dog Show

Annual doggie competition at Cobo Conference and Exhibition Center. See canines show off during demonstrations and competitions. Don't let anyone in the family try to pet the four-legged creatures, however, or you'll be scolded; trust me on this. (248) 352-7469 or www.detroitkennelclub.com.

Ann Arbor Film Festival

Annual event since 1963 featuring 16mm independent and experimental film. Might be best suited for older kids. (734) 995-5356 or www.aafilmfest.org.

Pow Wow at Chrysler Arena

An annual event since 1972, experience more than 1,000 Native American singers, dancers, drummers, and artisans as they gather for competitions. Ann Arbor, (734) 763-9044.

Appendix

April

Sugarloaf Art Fair

Hundreds of nationally recognized fine artists and contemporary craft designers, specialty foods, and live entertainment at the Novi Expo Center. (248) 348-5600 or www.sugarloafcrafts.com.

May

Greektown Arts Festival

This festival features 135 artists and craftspeople, jazz, blues, and gospel music. Located in the heart of Greektown in Detroit. (313) 963-3357.

Downtown Hoedown

Polish off your cowboy boots and head off to this free annual festival held in Hart Plaza on the Detroit River, featuring local and national country music acts and food. (734) 459-9157.

Detroit Electronic Music Festival

A three-day free festival of nonstop electronic music and dancing in Hart Plaza. (313) 392-9200 or www.electronicmusicfest.com.

A Parent's Guide to

Southeastern Michigan

Calendar

June

International Freedom Festival

A fifteen-day festival highlighted by a tug-of-war across the Detroit River, tugboat races, historical reenactments, and a huge fireworks display. (519) 252-7264 or **www.freedom-festival.com**.

Belleville Strawberry Festival

An annual event since 1976 featuring live entertainment, crafts show, parade, carnival rides and games, delectable strawberry treats, and the Lil' Miss Strawberry Princess Pageant. (734) 697-3137 or **www.nationalstrawberryfest.com**.

Ann Arbor Summer Festival

The annual outdoor and indoor extravaganza at the Power Center features local and nationally acclaimed performing artists. (734) 647-2278.

Michigan Challenge Balloonfest

More than fifty hot air balloons race. Includes a carnival, stunt kite flying, an arts festival, and an antique car show. Held at the Howell High School complex. (517) 546-3920.

Appendix

July

Ann Arbor Street Art Fairs

Crowds visit the Ann Arbor street art fairs each year.
Photo courtesy of Ann Arbor Area Convention and Visitors Bureau

Comprised of four juried art fairs in downtown Ann Arbor, this event boasts more than 500,000 visitors in a four-day period. The art fairs feature more than 1,200 artists, live performances, ethnic foods, street performers, and children's activity booths.
(734) 995-7281.

Calendar

Port Huron to Mackinac Island Yacht Race

More than 250 yachts participate in the largest freshwater sailing race in the U.S. See them off in Port Huron or greet the winners on Mackinac Island. (231) 759-8596 or **www.porthuronmackinac.com**.

Comerica TasteFest

Five days of munchies, music, and merchandise in Detroit's New Center area. More than 175 local restaurants and sixty local and national music acts participate. (313) 927-1101 or **www.tastefest.com**.

Arab and Chaldean Festival

The largest cultural event of its kind in the U.S., this three-day festival features food, a cultural exhibit gallery, and live entertainment. Held in Detroit's Hart Plaza. (248) 960-9956.

Seven Lakes State Park Balloon Festival

About thirty hot air balloons race in Holly to benefit local nonprofit organizations. (248) 634-9400.

Michigan Elvis Festival

Two days of hundreds of Elvis impersonators, Elvis' favorite food, and unimaginable amounts of King kitsch held at Frog Island Park in Ypsilanti. For unknown reasons, some people even decide to get married here! (734) 480-3974 or **www.mielvisfest.org**.

Saline Celtic Festival

With music, food, dancing, art, and haggis tossing. Saline, (734) 944-2810 or **www.salineceltic.org**.

Wayne County Fair

Auctions, animals, 4-H exhibits, merchants' tents, and carnival rides at the Wayne County Fairgrounds, on Quirk Road near Belleville. (734) 697-7002.

Appendix

August

Michigan State Fair

Since 1849, families enjoy rides, concerts, and educational exhibits at this enormous state fair (see Page 29 for additional info). (313) 369-8250.

Woodward Dream Cruise

The world's largest one-day car show runs along Woodward Avenue from Ferndale to Pontiac. More than 1.5 million people attend, so be prepared for crowds. (248) 288-4694 or **www.woodwarddreamcruise.com**.

About one million people come to the Detroit area for the annual Woodward Avenue Dream Cruise. Photo by Vito Palmisano

Calendar

Concours d'Elegance

High-end auto show featuring more than 200 vintage cars from 1900 to 1969 on the lawn of Meadowbrook Hall in Rochester. (248) 370-3140 or www.mbhconcours.org.

St. Andrew's Society of Detroit Highland Games

A tradition for more than 150 years, this Scottish group brings its Highland dancing, Celtic music, and caber toss competition to the Greenmead Historic Village in Livonia. (248) 333-3176 or www.highlandgames.com.

Fiesta Mexicana

Authentic food, music, and crafts held at Historic Fort Wayne in Detroit. (313) 554-9419.

African World Festival

This weekend-long event celebrates the cultural contributions of the African American community and features educational programs, music, art, and food. (313) 494-5824.

Nautical Mile Venetian Festival

In the lake community of St. Clair Shores, this event features a parade of decoratively lit boats, an arts and crafts show, concerts, a cardboard boat race, and a fireworks display. (586) 773-3624 or www.nauticalmile.org.

Appendix

September

Common Ground Sanctuary Art in the Park

More than 190 juried fine artists, live entertainment, and a hands-on children's art area. The event is the primary fundraiser for Common Ground Sanctuary, a twenty-four-hour nonprofit agency dedicated to helping youths, adults, and families in crisis. (248) 456-8150 or **www.ArtinthePark.info**.

Detroit Festival of the Arts

Set in a twenty-block area of Detroit's University Cultural Center, this festival boasts a juried fine arts show, music, dance, theatre, and a children's area. (313) 577-5088 or **www.detroitfestival.com**.

Ford Detroit International Jazz Festival

This free Labor Day weekend event brings to Hart Plaza more than 120 international and regional jazz musicians. (313) 963-7622 or **www.detroitjazzfest.com**.

Michigan Renaissance Festival

Celebrate amid armored, jousting knights and period artistry. (248) 634-5552 or **www.michrenfest.com**

Calendar

October

Zoo Boo at the Detroit Zoo

A "merry not scary" Halloween event geared toward kids ages 2–7. (248) 541-5835 or www.detroitzoo.org.

Oktoberfest

A Munich-style festival, complete with bratwurst, pretzels, gingerbread hearts, and German beer (for mom and dad), plus music, dancing, and kiddie rides. Held at Freedom Hill County Park in Sterling Heights, call (586) 979-7010.

November

America's Thanksgiving Day Parade

This nationally televised parade has brought families to brave the cold in downtown Detroit for more than seventy-five years. (313) 923-7400 or www.theparade.org.

Annual Jewish Book Fair

Each year this event brings the nation's hottest authors to the Jewish community centers in Oak Park and West Bloomfield, usually including a few children's book authors. (248) 661-1000.

Appendix

December

Wayne County Lightfest

A spectacular four-mile cruise down Hines Drive (from Westland to Dearborn Heights) featuring thirty-nine giant holiday displays and lots of lights. Usually runs from mid-November through January. (734) 261-1990.

Dickens Olde Fashioned Christmas Festival

Every weekend from Thanksgiving to Christmas families can mingle with characters out of Charles Dickens's Victorian novels in the quaint village of Holly. Visit antique and specialty shops and witness jugglers, traveling musicians, and carolers. (248) 634-1900.

New Year Jubilee of Southeastern Michigan

An alcohol- and drug-free celebration with music, dancing, singing, skits, clowns, magic, and more in Ypsilanti. (734) 483-4444.

Supplemental Area Directory

Music & Theatres

Cinema Café	4605 Cass	(313) 833-1944
Detroit Film Theatre at the DIA	5200 Woodward	(313) 833-2323
IMAX Dome Theatre at the Detroit Science Center	5020 John R	(313) 724-3623
Detroit Symphony Orchestra	3711 Woodward	(313) 576-5111
Detroit Women's Coffeehouse	4605 Cass	(313) 832-6980
The Majestic	4140 Woodward	(313) 833-9700
Masonic Temple	500 Temple	(313) 832-2232
Wayne State University—Bonstelle Theatre	3424 Woodward	(313) 577-2960
Wayne State University—Hilberry Theatre	4743 Cass	(313) 577-2400
Wayne State University—Community Arts Forum	5980 Cass	(313) 577-2400
Walk & Squawk / Furniture Factory	4126 Third	(313) 832-8890

Appendix

Restaurants, Cafes & Coffee Houses

American Grille (DIA)	5200 Woodward	(313) 833-1857
Avalon International Breads	422 W. Willis	(313) 832-0008
Baskin Robbins (WSU Campus)	5221 Gullen Mall	(313) 833-5631
Blimpies	108 W. Hancock	(313) 831-0711
Bush's Garden of Eating	3955 Woodward	(313) 831-6711
Cappy's Restaurant	5408 Woodward	(313) 871-9820
Cass Café	4620 Cass	(313) 831-1400
China One Buffet	3750 Woodward	(313) 832-1111
Circa 1890 Saloon	5474 Cass	(313) 831-1122
Duet (Orchestra Place)	3663 Woodward	(313) 831-3838
Epicurus Place	111 W. Warren	(313) 832-0133
Friar Tuck's (WSU campus)	5221 Gullen Mall	(313) 832-4760
Hannan House Coffee Shop	4750 Woodward	(313) 833-1840
Harmonie Garden Café	87 W. Palmer	(313) 831-4420
The Ice Cream Company	107 W. Warren	(313) 833-8948
Kresge Court Café (DIA)	5200 Woodward	(313) 833-1932
Lewis H. Latimer Café (Museum of African American History)	315 E. Warren	(313) 494-5882
Little Caesars (WSU campus)	5221 Gullen Mall	(313) 831-2590
Majestic Café and Theatre Center	4124 Woodward	(313) 833-9700
Mario's	4222 Second	(313) 832-1616
Olympian Cafe	119 W. Warren	(313) 647-9686
Small World Café (International Institute)	111 E. Kirby	(313) 874-2233
Subway	39 W. Warren	(313) 831-2190
Traffic Jam and Snug	511 W. Canfield	(313) 831-9470
Twingo's	4710 Cass	(313) 832-3832
Union Street	4145 Woodward	(313) 831-3965
The Whitney	4421 Woodward	(313) 832-5700

Supplemental Area Directory

Museums

Charles H. Wright Museum of African American History	315 E. Warren	(313) 494-5800
Detroit Historical Museum	5401 Woodward	(313) 833-1805
The Detroit Institute of Arts (DIA)	5200 Woodward	(313) 833-7900
Detroit Science Center	5020 John R	(313) 724-3623
Heritage Museum & Fine Arts Center	110 E. Ferry	(313) 871-1667
Wayne State University Museum of Anthropology	6005 Cass	(313) 577-2598

Galleries and Gift Shops

College for Creative Studies Center Galleries	301 Frederick	(313) 664-7800
Charles H. Wright Museum of African American History Gift Shop	315 E. Warren	(313) 494-5800
C-Pop Gallery	4160 Woodward	(313) 833-9901
Detroit Artists Market	4719 Woodward	(313) 832-8540
Detroit Historical Museum Old Detroit Shop	5401 Woodward	(313) 833-7911
The Detroit Institute of Arts Museum Shop	5200 Woodward	(313) 833-7944
Detroit Science Center Gift Shop	5020 John R	(313) 724-3623
Hannan Foundation Ellen Kayrod Gallery	4750 Woodward	(313) 833-1300
International Institute Gift Shop	111 E. Kirby	(313) 871-8600
The Scarab Club	217 Farnsworth	(313) 831-1250
Wayne State University Community Arts Gallery	5980 Cass	(313) 577-2203
Wayne State University Elaine L. Jacob Gallery	480 Hancock	(313) 577-2423

Appendix

Education

College for Creative Studies (CCS) College of Art & Design	201 E. Kirby	(313) 664-7440
CCS Continuing and Community Education	201 E. Kirby	(313) 664-7456
Center for Humanistic Studies— Graduate School of Psychology	40 E. Ferry	(313) 875-7400
Detroit Public Schools Headquarters	5057 Woodward	(313) 494-1000
Wayne State University (WSU)	6050 Cass	(313) 577-2424
Detroit Historical Society	5401 Woodward	(313) 833-7934
Detroit Public Library	5201 Woodward	(313) 833-1000
Friends of the Detroit Public Library	5201 Woodward	(313) 833-4048
The International Institute of Metropolitan Detroit	111 E. Kirby	(313) 871-8600
Preservation Wayne	4735 Cass	(313) 577-3559
Southeast Michigan Arts Forum	1008 Ferdinand	(313) 843-6940
University Cultural Center Association	4735 Cass	(313) 577-5088

Supplemental Area Directory

Health Care

Detroit Institute for Children	5447 Woodward	(313) 832-1100
Detroit Medical Center (DMC)	4201 St. Antoine	(313) 745-3603
DMC Corporate Headquarters	3663 Woodward	(313) 578-2500
Children's Hospital of Michigan	3901 Beaubien	(800) 666-3466
Detroit Receiving and University Health Center	4201 St. Antoine	(313) 745-3000
Harper Hospital	3990 John R	(313) 745-8040
Hutzel Hospital	4797 St. Antoine	(313) 745-7555
Rehabilitation Institute of MI.	261 Mack	(313) 745-9700
John D. Dingell VA Medical Center	4646 John R	(313) 576-1000
Karmanos Cancer Institute	4100 John R	(800) 527-6266
WSU School of Medicine	540 E. Canfield	(313) 577-1466

Religious

Cass Community United Methodist	3901 Cass	(313) 833-7730
Cathedral Church of St. Paul Herlong Cathedral School	4800 Woodward	(313) 831-5000
First Congregational Church	33 E. Forest	(313) 831-4080
First Unitarian Universalist Church	4605 Cass	(313) 833-9107

Public Safety

Detroit Police Department 13th Precinct	4747 Woodward	(313) 596-1300
Wayne State University	76 W. Hancock	(313) 577-6057
(Emergency)		(313) 577-2222

Appendix

Business

Bank One	3663 Woodward	(313) 831-3223
Bank One	5057 Woodward	(313) 833-1900
Comerica Bank	3750 Woodward	(313) 564-5717
National City Bank	4111 Woodward	(313) 832-4040
Charfoos & Christensen, P.C.	5510 Woodward	(313) 875-8080

Cultural

Art Center Music School	3975 Cass	(313) 832-1711
Center for Caribbean Arts and Culture	421 E. Ferry	(313) 438-3109

Social

American Red Cross	100 Mack	(313) 833-4440
Barat Child & Family Services		(313) 833-1525
Brush Park Development Corp.	2930 Woodward	(313) 833-4987
Cass Corridor Neighborhood Development Corp	3535 Cass	(313) 831-0199
The Children's Center	79 W. Alexandrine	(313) 831-5535
Detroit Assoc. of Women's Clubs	5461 Brush	(313) 873-1727
Detroit Neighborhood and Family Initiative	4750 Woodward	(313) 832-1201
Detroit Urban League	208 Mack	(313) 832-4600
Hannan House	4750 Woodward	(313) 833-1300
Hospice of Michigan	400 Mack	(313) 578-5000
Matrix Human Services	120 Parsons	(313) 831-1000
Detroit Omega Foundation, Inc.	235 E. Ferry	(313) 872-1646

A Parent's Guide to
Southeastern Michigan

Index

A

Index

Appendix

Index

Appendix

M

A Parent's Guide to
Southeastern Michigan

Index

N

O

P

Appendix

Index

Appendix

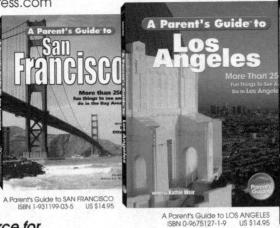

A Parent's Guide to
First Aid

ISBN: 1-931199-20-5

Price: US$17.95 (CAN$26.95)

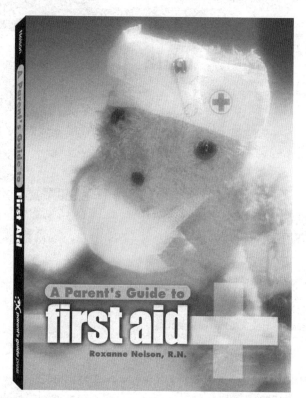

- **When something goes wrong**, Parents and Caregivers are often the first ones on the scene. Knowledge of fundamental First Aid principles can be vital for the health of children. While nothing can replace qualified First Aid training, this book can provide an essential reference in time of need.

- **Common childhood mishaps** are listed in alphabetical order – from Allergic Reactions to Vomiting – for quick reference. Symptoms and causes are clearly explained by former pediatric and newborn intensive care nurse Roxanne Nelson to help caregivers understand the situation.

- **Step by step instructions** help caregivers determine the appropriate level of care and when to seek it – from a call to 911 in the direst circumstances or giving First Aid that can be undertaken at home.

- **Accident prevention** is the best First Aid one can give. The book includes common sense prevention tips for each situation, as well as general safety precautions parents can take around the home.

- **Chapters devoted to CPR/Rescue Breathing**, the Heimlich maneuver, and the emergency medical system each help parents and caregivers learn the basics before a crisis arises – helping them stay calm and in control of the situation.

- **What to stock in an effective home First Aid Kit**, where to keep it, and how to keep it up-to-date.

- **Indexed**.

parent's guide press

PO Box 461730
Los Angeles CA 90046
phone: 800-549-6646
fax: 323-782-1775

A Parent's Guide to
Money

ISBN: 1-931199-19-1

Price: US$19.95 (CAN$29.95)

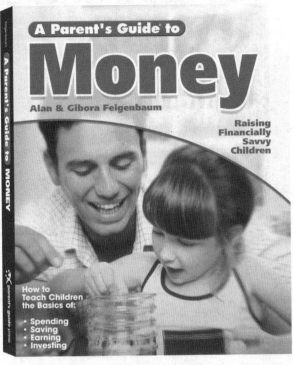

• **The collegiate class just entering the job market** carries the highest level of student and credit-card debt ever, even considering inflation. These recent graduates will have to learn for themselves how to responsibly manage money, but there's plenty of time to ensure that kids growing up today can enter adulthood better prepared than their older siblings were.

• **Financial writer Alan Feigenbaum,** with the help of daughter Gibora, shows how to view children's financial development the same way a parent might view their growth stages – the financial equivalents of crawling, standing, then walking. Picture-book to checkbook, car seat buying to buying that first car, *A Parent's Guide to Money* leads parents through the necessary baby steps on the road to family financial success.

• **How parents can prepare their personal finances** when they're expecting. Starting with difficult questions about false, 'pre-conceived,' assumptions about managing money, and where those may have been learned, Alan helps parents get their pre-child finances under control in preparation for keeping the same control after baby has arrived.

• **When to introduce children to financial concepts** – from the first piggy bank through investing in mutual funds. Once infants understand that money is more than something to put in their mouths, it's time to start teaching them what money is, what it's for, and how to control it (rather than it controlling them later).

• **Tips and strategies** to teach children what they need to know about the four basics: Spending, Earning, Saving, and Investing. The thorough discussions of these four topics make clear many financial concepts many parents may themselves be confused about. The authors then provide scores of intriguing suggestions about how and when to teach the same concepts to children.

• **A thorough Resource Appendix** leads readers to scores of online resources – games, calculators, and in depth information – all reviewed by the authors for accuracy and relevance.

• **Indexed**.

parent's guide press

PO Box 461730
Los Angeles CA 90046
phone: 800-549-6646
fax: 323-782-1775

A Parent's Guide to

School Projects

ISBN: 1-931199-08-6

Price: US$17.95 (CAN$26.95)

- **Children in today's public and private schools face far different requirements than their parents faced just a generation ago.** Today's classrooms require more homework (at an earlier age), a more highly developed sense of design and creativity, and more commitment of time and effort from students and parents. Nothing reflects this change more than the growing reliance on project-oriented teaching.

- *A Parent's Guide to School Projects* **introduces parents to this new educational world.** Beginning in Kindergarten, students are required to put together a variety of projects, from the familiar Science Project to interesting alternatives to the book report. Author Kathie Weir shares insights gained from her experience coaching her own children through scores of projects. Her experience as an educator allows her to offer perspective from the other side.

- **The book features examples of successful projects in several subjects** including Science, History, English and Geography. Kathie also offers tips and general guidelines on writing research papers and putting together effective student presentations.

- **The new emphasis on projects is not limited to those designed for individual students.** Group Projects are increasingly popular with teachers as a way to introduce students to group dynamics. A Parent's Guide to School Projects offers advice on how to avoid the most common pitfalls. Among these are lack of coordination among participants and the unfortunate occasions when a minority of the membership ends up doing the majority of the work.

- **Classroom projects tell only half the story.** Just as teachers seek ways to enhance and enliven classroom activities, teachers and administrators try to encourage closer parent involvement beyond helping their children with their homework. From field trip chaperone to Parent Teacher Association President to sponsoring after-school activities, parents are offered plenty of opportunities to help in both public and private schools.

- **As Public Schools strain to meet increasing demands on limited resources, they've come to rely upon a variety of fundraisers to help defray their costs.** Kathie's been involved in dozens of these fundraisers, and she offers advice and guidance for every level of participation — parents helping their children sell 'School Spirit knick-knacks' and those proposing and coordinating entire fundraisers will benefit.

- **Sometimes fundraising is not enough** — public schools appreciate contributions of expertise and experience from everybody in the community as a way to enrich learning. A Parent's Guide to School Projects explores these possibilities for greater involvement, from giving a talk on 'Career Day' to organizing a three-day 'Harvest Festival' to teach city children about farm life.

- **An appendix collects sample project assignments** — contributed by elementary and middle school teachers.

- **Indexed for easy reference**. Includes a glossary.

About the Author: Kathie Weir, mother of a 12-year-old and 14-year-old, has spent the last nine years coaching her children through increasingly complex school projects, papers, and presentations. She has served as a PTO board member, helped out in the classroom, and coordinated scores of fundraisers and extra-curricular activities. Her experience as an active volunteer parent and substitute teacher has brought her into contact with dozens of dedicated public school teachers, many of whom contributed project assignments as well as their insight. Kathie is also the author of **A Parent's Guide to Los Angeles** and has published numerous articles and essays about children and child rearing.

parent's guide press

PO Box 461730
Los Angeles CA 90046
phone: 800-549-6646
fax: 323-782-1775